THE RO

Quiet Influence

Diane Strack, General Editor
Authors: Debbie Brunson, Jeana Floyd, Donna Gaines,
Susie Hawkins, Diane Strack, Lisa Young

NAVPRESS

NAVPRESS⊘.

NavPress is the publishing ministry of The Navigators, an international Christian organization and leader in personal spiritual development. NavPress is committed to helping people grow spiritually and enjoy lives of meaning and hope through personal and group resources that are biblically rooted, culturally relevant, and highly practical.

For a free catalog go to www.NavPress.com
or call 1.800.366.7788 in the United States or 1.800.839.4769 in Canada.

Cover design by Arvid Wallen
Cover image by Shutterstock

General Editor: Diane Strack
Authors: Debbie Brunson, Jeana Floyd, Donna Gaines, Susie Hawkins, Diane Strack, Lisa Young

Some of the anecdotal illustrations in this book are true to life and are included with the permission of the persons involved. All other illustrations are composites of real situations, and any resemblance to people living or dead is coincidental.

Unless otherwise identified, all Scripture quotations in this publication are taken from the New King James Version (NKJV). Copyright © 1982 by Thomas Nelson, Inc. Used by permission. All rights reserved. Other versions used include: the *Holy Bible, New International Version*® (NIV®), Copyright © 1973, 1978, 1984 by International Bible Society, used by permission of Zondervan, all rights reserved; *THE MESSAGE* (MSG). Copyright © 1993, 1994, 1995, 1996, 2000, 2001, 2002. Used by permission of NavPress Publishing Group; the *Holy Bible*, New Living Translation (NLT), copyright © 1996, 2004. Used by permission of Tyndale House Publishers, Inc., Wheaton, Illinois 60189. All rights reserved; the New American Standard Bible® (NASB), Copyright © 1960, 1962, 1963, 1968, 1971, 1972, 1973, 1975, 1977, 1995 by The Lockman Foundation. Used by permission; and the King James Version (KJV).

Printed in the United States of America

2 3 4 5 6 7 8 / 13 12 11 10 09

Contents

INTRODUCTION

by Diane Strack

Standing in line at the grocery store can be enough to give you a serious attack of insecurity. Magazine covers call out to women: "Lose weight. Make money. Save money. Budget your time and your finances. Organize yourself and worry less. Reduce your risk of cancer. Lift your face. Make over your body. Clean your house better, cook faster, and don't forget: Be a great lover while you're at it!"

While every television show, magazine, and Internet ad offers an opinion on how you can improve, make over, or "fix" yourself, the Bible gives this timeless advice:

> Take your everyday, ordinary life—your sleeping, eating, going-to-work, and walking-around life—and place it before God as an offering. Embracing what God does for you is the best thing you can do for him. Don't become so well-adjusted to your culture that you fit into it without even thinking. Instead, fix your attention on God. You'll be changed from the inside out. Readily recognize what he wants from you, and quickly respond to it. Unlike the culture around you, always dragging you down to its level of immaturity, God brings the best out of you, develops well-formed maturity in you. (Romans 12:1-2, MSG)

Now that's better than a makeover.

There is a popular phrase that says, "The more things change, the more they remain the same." This sentence describes the hearts of women over the last four thousand years. Everyday, ordinary lives offered to God with personal sacrifice and commitment have written legacies throughout history that changed their own cultures as well as generations after them. In this study, we'll peer into the culture and community of six influential women and highlight their personalities and characteristics.

These women are not much different from you or me: They faced family conflicts, economic concerns, personal insecurities, fear of the future, and strong cultural and moral issues. One characteristic we see in each of these women is an intense desire to please God by offering her life—every aspect—to the will of God according to Romans 12:1: "Therefore, I urge you, brothers, in view of God's mercy, to offer your bodies as living sacrifices, holy and pleasing to God—this is your spiritual act of worship" (NIV). As you study these women, you will notice they were not famous in their day but rather ordinary. In each of their stories, you will see a moment in which they made a decision to live unwaveringly for Christ, regardless of the cost. This presentation of self makes them memorable even to this day and well into the future.

Presentation Is Everything

When doctors suspected another blockage in my artery, I asked if I could stay awake during my heart surgery. I was in denial and wanted to see the damage for myself. I wanted to watch it be fixed, a choice I might not make again if given the chance. The cold reality of listening to their discussions and watching the doctor probe my arteries and heart on a large screen brought gripping fear instead of the understanding I had hoped for.

My first thought was, *Be careful in there!* My second was, *Stop it!* The process was so overwhelming that I couldn't speak. I could only watch and listen. Tears leaked down my cheeks. I can't even begin to describe the feeling of utter helplessness that engulfed me. Seeing the damage, I knew that my life could have been over within seconds, yet I had graciously been given another chance to live. Silently, I cried within, *Lord, meet me here. I need You here and now.* Almost immediately a great peace engulfed me, and I heard the voice of God. I know the doctor and the nurses didn't hear it, but He wasn't speaking to them—He was speaking to me. He simply said, "Present yourself to Me. I'll do the rest."

I learned in that moment that presenting myself wholly and completely to Him was the plan He had for me all along. By surrendering to Him, I finally felt strong and peaceful. In trusting Him, I was able to be confident about my future. While the doctors were working on my physical heart, the Lord was transforming my inner heart. I came away from that experience focused on serving God rather than dwelling on my challenges. Romans 12:1 came alive in me, and I was transformed into a woman of peace and faith—a gift from God I will always be grateful for.

The word *present* is from the Greek *paristemi* and means "to stand beside, be at hand, and be ready." Its most significant translation is "to yield out of strength," not out of weakness. While some translations of Romans 12:1 say, "Present your bodies," it is clear that Paul was speaking of the total person: body, mind, spirit, and even personality. The totality of who you are, every day, in every action.

At the time Paul wrote this letter, the Romans were familiar with pagan practices of immorality with temple prostitutes. "Present your body" was certainly a vivid and easily understood phrase for that culture. We are reminded from this verse that the actions of the body come from within the mind and heart. We cannot separate them.

True surrender to Christ begins with praise. In Romans 11:33-36, Paul declared the wonder and riches of the mercy of God, available to anyone and everyone. He said that this is "unsearchable," meaning that we can find no beginning or end to it. It existed before man and will exist after man. Because of the riches of God's mercy, let us present ourselves to Him.

Present Yourself to the One
Who Is Worthy of Praise

Praise is a natural response to understanding the majesty of who God is and what He does. Note the personal experience of the apostle Paul as he broke into praise in the following verses:

> Oh, the depth of the riches both of the wisdom and knowledge of God! How unsearchable are His judgments and His ways past finding out!

> "For who has known the mind of the LORD?
> Or who has become His counselor?"
> "Or who has first given to Him
> And it shall be repaid to him?"

> For of Him and through Him and to Him are all things, to whom be glory forever. Amen. (Romans 11:33-36)

Most of us will agree that praise and worship in our contemporary services are important; in fact, they were modeled in Scripture. But we should be careful not to substitute this for intimate, private worship. Our congregational worship should be an overflow of all that God is doing personally and privately within us. It should be a culmination of what is happening in our prayer lives, not the reverse.

Praise is what happens when a "seeking of the mind turns to adoration of the heart."
— William Barclay

8

When we stop thinking about what we're capable of and what others think of us and instead focus on the wonder and majesty of who He is, we enter into true worship. We hear another voice, the voice of God. Paul said that this type of worship is our "reasonable" (or in the Greek, our "logical") service to Him. In other words, once we enter into an understanding of His majesty, once we enter into private, overflowing worship, the next logical or perhaps the only reasonable thing to do is to present ourselves to Him.

Presenting yourself to God transcends both the terrible and the ordinary. It moves you beyond a life of adjusting to problems and circumstances and takes you into an intimacy with the Savior so great that it cannot be explained but must be experienced. If you present yourself to God, He will meet you with such transforming power that you are able to rise above and beyond the clamor of the culture and pursue His heavenly call on your life.

Throughout history, God has called women to an all-consuming act of worship. When these women obediently presented their whole hearts to God, He blessed the simple act of submission and multiplied it into a remarkable legacy for all generations. Could He do this in your life? Dare to trust Him, present yourself, and join the adventure of being a Romans 12:1 woman.

Chapter 1

Deborah

Courage and Leadership

by Jeana Floyd

Culture and Background

1250–1150 BC

During the time of the judges, the average life span was around thirty-five years. Family was very important because ancient Israel was an agrarian society, and extended families helped support and provide for one another. Marriages were arranged by the bride's father or legal guardian. A woman's father gave the husband a dowry, and the husband-to-be paid a bride price to the father. Tradition required that the dowry be one-tenth of the father's estate. A woman moved into her husband's household, and her greatest worth was in bearing many children.[1] Barrenness was considered one of the greatest tragedies a woman could suffer, and often a husband would divorce his wife if she were barren. Within this patriarchal society, sons were preferred over daughters because sons remained with their families when married but daughters moved to live with their new families.

Several laws outlined in the Bible offered special protection or instructions for women. For example, under the purity laws in Leviticus, a woman was considered impure or unclean for seven days during menstruation and whatever she touched was considered unclean. This provided her a break from housework, caring for children, and sexual relations with her husband. Also, both men and women were to be executed if they committed adultery, but only men were allowed to divorce their wives.[2]

Women traditionally wore tunics of wool, cotton, or linen with an outer garment that went to the ground. They wore veils covering their hair, and if unmarried, many women wore veils over their faces. Leather sandals were the most common type of footwear. Jewish women wore many pieces of jewelry on their wrists, ankles, and ears, and they used makeup and perfume.[3]

Two women in the Old Testament book of Judges defined courage for all the ages. Their personal lives differed, but their circumstances were the same. They had little to offer but themselves, and that's exactly what the Lord desired. He needed nothing else. Deborah—a wife, prophetess, counselor, and judge—and Jael, a humble Bedouin woman dwelling in a tent, were two ordinary women used by God to deliver the Jews from the hand of a mighty enemy. Let's look at how God used those women. Hopefully, it will stir a fire of courage within you that will allow you to overcome sin, temptation, and the challenges of our culture.

Daily I, Deborah, wife of Lapidoth and judge of Israel, made my way through the hot sand to the oasis of date palms in the desert for a change of view, for a quiet and gentle time to listen in the hope that Yahweh would once again speak. Israel had been in bondage for twenty years, and the refreshing tree allowed me to think, pray, and hope in Him. Our poverty was great; village life ceased; the people turned to pagan gods; and hope had become as scarce as food.

Then one day, something strange happened: People started coming to the tree and inquiring what I was doing alone every day. I explained that I came to worship Yahweh, the one true God, and to listen for His voice. They were intrigued by this and asked about His Law, and I began to tell them what I learned from the scrolls and the prophets. Daily I watched as more and more people came, and one day I was addressed as Deborah, the prophetess who judges Israel. The people continued to come, seeking answers and peace, and I marveled that they would ask a woman to speak about Yahweh's words.

On one of my early mornings under the palm tree, before anyone else arrived, I was startled by a voice. My heart leapt within me for I knew it was the voice of Yahweh, and I fell to the ground, bowing before Him. He spoke, and I listened in awe. "Wake up, wake up, Deborah! Wake up, wake up, and break out in song! Call Barak to arise and together take captive." I could scarcely believe that He had spoken after so many years of silence and that He had spoken to me, a woman! A word from Yahweh after twenty years of bondage—hope in the midst of utter despair. And then I shuddered in doubt: "How can I persuade a people who worship pagan gods, who have no weapons or the will with which to fight, and who do not believe Yahweh would speak to a woman about war to willingly offer themselves?"

He had said to call Barak, and so I obeyed, daring to hope, daring to believe that He would use me, that He would deliver this people from the enemy. And Barak believed me! He had one condition: "If you go with me, I will go; but if you don't go with me, I won't go." So I agreed.

Word spread that Yahweh had spoken to Deborah and that Barak would lead the Israelites. Soon ten thousand men from the tribes of Zebulun and Naphtali gathered and followed with us. There was no turning back now—Sisera gathered together nine hundred iron chariots, ten thousand traditional chariots, three hundred thousand foot soldiers, and ten thousand cavalry to meet us at the Kishon River. It was a fierce sight.

Remembering the word of Yahweh, I was filled with boldness as I sang, "March on, my soul; be strong!" To Barak, I urged: "Go! This is the day the Lord has given Sisera into your hands. Has not the Lord gone ahead of you?" So Barak went down to Mount Tabor, followed by the ten thousand men with willing hearts. What happened next was astonishing. The Lord Himself routed all of the enemy's chariots and armies so that Sisera abandoned his chariot and fled on foot. But Barak pursued them, and the troops of Sisera *fell by the sword. Not a man was left as the stars fought from heaven and the age-old river Kishon swept them away. The flash floods were replaced with sunshine just as utter despair was overcome by joy in the gates.*

Barak and I could not contain our praise, and we began to sing: "When the princes in Israel take the lead, when the people willingly offer themselves—praise the Lord! O Lord, may all your enemies perish! But may they who love you be like the sun when it rises in its strength." (See Judges 4–5.)[4]

Courage: from Latin *cor*, meaning "heart."
— *Merriam-Webster Dictionary*

Deborah's Personal Presentation

It is significant that the word *courage* has the word *heart* as its root. As we see by the boldness of Deborah, courage comes forth from the core of one's beliefs, that which defines our reason for living and fills the heart to overflowing. Because of this full heart, we are moved to unwavering action in the name of what is good and right.

The nation of Israel found itself under the oppression of King Jabin of Hazor, a Canaanite king. Judges 4:1 states that "the children of Israel again did evil in the sight of the LORD," and this oppression was the direct result of Israel's refusal to follow the laws of God. Judges 5 describes life in Israel during those days. Its civil court was inept, its military weak and scattered: "Not a shield or spear could be seen among forty thousand warriors in Israel!" (verse 8, NLT). Israel could not and would not defend its border, and the priesthood was ineffective as the people worshipped pagan idols: "Israel chose new gods" (verse 8, NLT). The life Yahweh planned seemed only a memory, and even normal life was no longer possible: "People avoided the main roads, and travelers stayed on winding pathways. There were few people left in the villages of Israel—until Deborah arose as a mother for Israel" (verses 6-7, NLT).

Sisera, the commander of Jabin's army, ruled ruthlessly over Israel for twenty years, and his nine hundred iron chariots frightened Israel, who had no weapons of any kind. The situation appeared hopeless.

Deborah, a woman of influence, went about her days taking care of business at home in the hill country of Ephraim. She began first as a counselor, and there under the large palm tree near her home, she became a judge. As a prophetess, Deborah drew people to the Word of God as she tried to bring order to the Israelites. Her leadership grew as the people's respect for her grew. It's noteworthy that availability to others and to her God was her greatest attribute. She rose to the challenge when God called her, and that decision led her to be victorious as she trusted God and inspired others within her sphere of influence with that same trust.

Her Ordinary Background and Extraordinary Call

- Deborah was first referred to as "the wife of Lapidoth" (Judges 4:4).
- In the same verse, Deborah was also referred to as a prophetess.
- Deborah was the only woman judge in the Old Testament. It is extremely significant that Deborah was chosen to serve as a judge in a male-dominant society.
- Deborah referred to herself as "a mother for Israel" (Judges 5:7, NLT). It is not clear whether this is a reference to her own offspring or an expression of her spiritual motherhood toward every son or daughter of Israel.[5]

Deborah: Hebrew word meaning "bee or wasp"; one Hebrew scholar described her in this colorful way: "She was a bee in peace and a wasp in war!"

— *The Believer's Study Bible*

Deborah's reputation as a counselor gained the confidence of the people of Israel. As she sought Yahweh on a daily basis under the palm tree, others carefully observed her communion. Her testimony of consistent worship and joy in the midst of difficult, depressing days brought the people of Israel to her for judgment.

CONSIDER THIS: What about Deborah qualified her to be chosen as a judge in Israel? What qualified her to call Barak to war? What attributes in your life could qualify you to be a woman of influence? Does your daily walk and reputation with Christ draw others to you for counsel or advice? When others come to you, are you ready to act as a prophetess—that is, one who proclaims the Word of God rather than a personal or cultural opinion? Are you faithfully going to God for personal needs and interceding for the needs of others?

An Unusual Call of Opportunity

Because of Deborah's faithfulness, the people elevated her to judge and prophetess, but it was her personal faith that gave her the courage to accept God's unusual call on her life. Deborah was awakened to action by the atrocities suffered by her people. Four times in Judges 5:12, the Lord called her to "wake up" (Hebrew: `uwr): "Wake up, Deborah, wake up! Wake up, wake up, and sing a song! Arise, Barak! Lead your captives away, son of Abinoam!" (NLT). Perhaps the message was, "Stop wishing and daydreaming about victory. Get up, get excited, and engage yourself fully. It's time to go for it! This is the Lord's day, and He will give us victory!"

Deborah was called to stir the heart of Barak. Though Barak was called to lead, it was Deborah's initial reaction to God's call that caused Barak to believe and the ten thousand Israelite men to follow.

After agonizing over the treatment of the Israelites, Deborah called Barak and delivered the command of the Lord, the God of Israel, to fight against Sisera. God called Deborah to:

- Give up the comfort of the palm tree to go to the battlefield
- Go against culture by delivering God's message to a man, risking ridicule and rebuke
- Obey the call of God regardless of the opinion of others
- Trust that God's power is more than enough to compensate for a lack of weapons, food, supplies, man power, and training

Deborah obeyed God and instructed Barak to get up and lead the army. The power of this narrative is seen in Deborah's faithful presentation before Yahweh—not only as she served as counselor, prophetess, and judge on a daily basis but also as she willingly delivered a message from God to Barak and boldly proclaimed victory *in advance.*

Courage Sometimes Needs a Friend

More than eighteen years ago, I was diagnosed with breast cancer. I did not understand why this happened to me, but I trusted God enough to know that He was about to lead me on a path of deeper faith as I watched Him unfold an uncertain future. Throughout the journey, I learned that God asks us to let go of our agendas and our ideal visions for a picture-perfect life so that He can work His perfect plan in our lives. While God asks us to let go, He never lets go of us. I am quite sure Deborah learned this as well as she faced difficult circumstances and an unknown future. I was often reminded that God is never surprised or caught off guard, not even by cancer, and that every needle that stuck me went through Him first. I was not alone. Cancer put God's Word to the test, and God's Word stood up every time. Courageous faith in my life now means:

- Being totally, helplessly dependent on God
- Trusting Him when things are beyond my control
- Knowing He is in control and I'm not
- Trusting Him when I'm afraid

- Trusting Him for the future and the unknown
- Knowing I will spend eternity with Him because I have placed my total trust in Jesus alone[6]

We know that God uses relationships in our lives to strengthen and encourage us, particularly in times of great testing. In the case of Deborah and Barak in Judges, it appears Barak was waiting for a partner, and he refused to go without Deborah: "Barak told her, 'I will go, but only if you go with me'" (Judges 4:8, NLT).

Deborah agreed to go with him, but she warned him that he would "receive no honor in this venture, for the LORD's victory over Sisera will be at the hands of a woman" (verse 9, NLT). It was disgraceful for a man to die at the hands of a woman during that time, making the significance of Barak's decision enormous. In verse 14, "Deborah said to Barak, 'Get ready! This is the day the LORD will give you victory over Sisera, for the LORD is marching ahead of you.' So Barak led his 10,000 warriors down the slopes of Mount Tabor into battle" (NLT).

Barak believed Deborah because he knew her reputation of consistency and confident faith. In Hebrews 11:32, Barak is listed as a man of faith, but in Judges he is a man dependent upon Deborah for victory. Deborah had courage to act upon the message she received from God. Barak needed someone to share the challenge with him. Sometimes we are called to be the catalyst for others to believe in a challenging time. Deborah was willing to be that.

CONSIDER THIS: Can you think of anyone you have encouraged by word or testimony to trust God for something difficult? Have you encouraged someone to believe and seen his or her life changed? What would it take for that to happen?

God used two women, Deborah and Jael, to deliver the Jews. Whatever Barak's weaknesses, God still honored him for his faith. When God speaks, how willing are you to follow His plan, even if it doesn't fit into your thinking?

Courage Is Rewarded with Victory

The battle took place by the waters of Megiddo where the Kishon River flowed down from Mount Tabor. Normally, the Kishon River is dry, but God sent a great storm that flooded the riverbed and trapped the iron chariots as they were coming down from Mount Tabor (see Judges 4:3; 5:20-22). Sisera and his army thought their iron chariots would give them victory, but they actually led to their defeat as the storm turned the plain into a swamp. Israel won a great battle that day, planned by God's revelation to Deborah and led by Barak.

Remember Deborah's prophecy: "The LORD will hand Sisera over to a woman" (Judges 4:9, NIV). That was okay with Barak as long as Deborah joined him in the battle. Her testimony gave him confidence and courage.

Sisera saw the flood coming, abandoned his army, and fled on foot. Hailed a great leader by his people, he showed his cowardice when things got tough on the battlefield. Sisera bailed and headed to the tent of Jael, the wife of Heber the Kenite (see verse 17). Heber had made peace with King Jabin and might have even helped him develop his powerful chariots. What we don't know is whether or not this was a willing alliance or if Heber had no choice in the matter.

A Hostile Hostess

Jael invited Sisera into her tent and told him not to fear. She gave him a drink and covered him (see verses 19-20). Traditionally, this was the strongest pledge of protection possible.[7] Sisera asked for water, but Jael exceeded his request by giving him a jug of milk, covering him, and promising to guard the door. Sisera fearfully fled his troops and hid and fearlessly trusted the sheltering hand of a humble woman. Not only did Jael use her skills to entice him into her tent to rest his weary body from the battlefield, but she also used her expertise of hammering down tent pegs from her Bedouin lifestyle. Using her own working tools—a peg and hammer—Jael drove a tent peg into Sisera's temple, killing her guest.

A rarity occurs in this story: Jael went against her place in society, her duties as a hostess, and her obligation to maintain her husband's neutrality in order to rescue God's people from the oppression of the Canaanites.[8] Her decision to side with the Israelites instead of the Canaanites, her husband's allies, was highly significant. Such action suggests that she placed her heart's commitment to God above all else.[9]

CONSIDER THIS: Courage is the power to do God's will regardless of the cost. The cost may be anything from personal ambition to the public approval of others. What keeps you from moving forward against the opinion of others or the customs of the culture?

The Result of Presentation: Victory

Not only was Deborah faithful to God's call of courage, she was quite articulate in her narrative of the Lord's victory in Judges 5, where she offered a beautiful song of praise. No wonder people stood in line to hear her advice. She defined leadership with clarity when she wrote, "When leaders lead in Israel . . . the people willingly offer themselves" (verse 2).

In her victory chant, Deborah boldly proclaimed the truth that many tribes had let a woman go into battle rather than take up their own swords. She honored those who had joined her—the tribes of Naphtali, Zebulun, and Issachar—for their bravery. However, she also named some of the tribes who were too cowardly to fight. Here again, we see another example of Deborah's courage to speak truth, even to the point of naming those who were unwilling to participate in the battle.

Deborah praised Jael's deed, knowing that it added to the shame of those who had quaked in fear as God used the women of Israel to drive away their enemies. She wanted the men of Israel to know that God uses humble, brave hearts.

Finally, we see two women, Deborah and Jael, rejoicing in victory as Sisera's mother weeps in sorrow. No one imagined that the Israelites would be the victors, and the news of Sisera's death and the utter defeat of his men must have sent shock waves through the people of Canaan.[10] God did it, and He used two women with willing hearts.

CONSIDER THIS: What are some reasons that cause people not to participate in a battle and sit on the sidelines instead? What brings you to the point of being willing to participate? Which reasons demonstrate courage? Which ones demonstrate cowardice?

Chapter 2

Mary, the Mother of Jesus

Enduring Faith

by Diane Strack

Culture and Background

15 BC–35 AD[1]

In the first century AD, three out of every ten Jewish children died before the age of eighteen, though the number was higher for non-Jewish people, probably due to the purity laws of the Jewish people. The average life span was forty to forty-five years, and unlike today, when women outlive men, a woman's average life span was about ten years shorter than a man's.

Houses were all-purpose one- or two-room squares with dirt floors, flat roofs, and wooden doorways. People slept on mats and owned very limited personal goods. A woman's daily job included preparing food for her family (grinding grain, baking bread, milking animals, making cheese). A family usually ate two meals a day, and food was served in a common bowl and eaten by dipping one's fingers into the bowl. Women had three garments of clothing: a tunic (the undergarment), a mantle or cloak (the outer garment), and a veil worn over her hair. Jewish boys began formal education at age five, but girls learned at home from their mothers and other women.

Men were the spiritual and legal heads of the house, and marriages were arranged by parents. Women, if they learned to read, were allowed to read the

Scripture but never in a public assembly. They could also form or participate in *minyans* (prayer groups with other women). Worship was conducted in synagogues, and it has long been believed that women were separated within the synagogue in women's galleries similar to the court of the women in ancient temple worship. As Jesus began His ministry, the fact that He taught women, allowed women to financially support His ministry, and ministered to women was seen as radical by the Jewish culture. Women at the time were seen more as second-class citizens.[2]

Mary, an unknown young Jewish girl, was chosen to give birth to, love, protect, teach, and raise Immanuel, "God with us." The bookends of her significant life have been portrayed in various art forms for centuries. Though countless nativities portray the joy and wonder of a new mother cradling her babe, the unique *Pietá* by Michelangelo gives us a dramatic understanding of her sorrow as she once again held her Son in her arms, this time lifeless. Mary lived dependent upon intense courage and deep, passionate faith.

Mary's life of adventure and faith began with a wondrous announcement, followed by angelic serenades and visits by strangers. But this awe was quickly darkened by the prophecy of Simeon when Jesus was presented as a child at the temple: "A sword will pierce through your own soul" (Luke 2:35). Challenging emotions continued to wreak havoc in Mary's heart throughout Jesus' life: the fear of the future, the loneliness of Bethlehem, the joy of birth, the strangeness of pagan Egypt, the pain of watching Jesus leave home, the joy of His miracles, the torture of the angry crowd and the beatings, the peace of trusting God, and the pain of watching Jesus hang between life and death in agony. Jesus had to endure the sins of the world, and Mary could do nothing to help.

Mary's every breath was sustained by faith as she faced joy and pain no other mother has known or will ever know. Mary isn't listed among those at the grave; perhaps it was more than she could endure.

She relied on the angel's salutation, "Do not be afraid" (Luke 1:30), and her Son's teaching, "Let not your heart be troubled; you believe in God, believe also in Me" (John 14:1). Believing was all that had sustained her until that moment, and she dared to wait on His resurrection—the purpose He often spoke of and that the prophets had foretold. She was, of course, rewarded with victory.

It's not fair! probably crossed Mary's mind more than once, but her legacy of enduring faith and courage will inspire lives until He comes again.

Chosen for Presentation

My lifelong fascination with angels is one reason that the story of the angel Gabriel's appearance to Mary is a favorite for me. I seek out paintings, books, and visuals that depict that moment when Gabriel (also my sweet grandson's name) appeared to the young, humble maiden and said, "Rejoice, highly favored [Greek: *charis*] one, the Lord is with you; blessed are you among women!" (Luke 1:28). What qualified this humble maiden to be chosen as the mother of the Son of God? Gabriel defined her credentials: She was one who "found favor" with God (Luke 1:30).

God is still looking for people who can be described as "finding favor [good will, pleasure] with God." It could be you. For most of us, we can't imagine the Lord calling us "favored one." Yet, in His Word He assures us that we can be. Because of His great love for us, the Lord has provided the plan by which we can be called a *charis* woman, one of grace and favor.

> Let not mercy and truth forsake you;
> Bind them around your neck,
> Write them on the tablet of your heart,
> And so find favor and high esteem
> In the sight of God and man. (Proverbs 3:3-4)

Solomon, the author of this proverb, spoke of a lovely necklace worn elegantly near the heart for all to see. This piece of jewelry is suitable for every outfit and every occasion; it is beautifully set with two jewels: the jewel of mercy (Hebrew: *checed*), goodness, kindness, and faithfulness; and the jewel of truth (Hebrew: *'emeth*), reliability, faithfulness, stability, and consistency.

These two qualities are to be worn around the neck, easily seen and apparent to all who meet us. They are to be the adornment of our character and our lives. Only then can we find favor with God and with man.

Adornment is also discussed by the apostle Peter in the New Testament:

> Do not let your adornment be merely outward—arranging the hair, wearing gold, or putting on fine apparel—rather let it be the hidden person of the heart, with the incorruptible beauty of a gentle and quiet spirit, which is very precious in the sight of God. (1 Peter 3:3-4)

Note that Peter didn't address what types of adornment; instead he defined the word. The favored woman of God is careful to choose inner adornment over outward appearance, understanding the power of her heart. The importance of this "gentle spirit" can be understood only in light of the word *precious*, which in the Greek means "of high value or price." God has placed great value on the *spirit* of women.

Spirit: "the rational spirit, the power by which the human being feels, thinks, decides."

— Strong's Exhaustive Concordance of the Bible and the Greek Dictionary of the New Testament

---

God's words about the value of women — *heart, spirit, gentle, hidden person* — contrast with the words our culture uses concerning women. Virtually every women's magazine is filled with articles about outward beauty. Although this is not wrong, perhaps it's not the best thing and certainly not the appropriate focus of a godly woman's life.

To be women of influence we must build our lives on mercy and truth. Paul wrote in Romans 12:2 to "be transformed by the renewing of your mind." He also gave us a plan on how to focus our thoughts:

> Whatever things are true, whatever things are noble, whatever things are just, whatever things are pure, whatever things are lovely, whatever things are of good report, if there is any virtue and if there is anything praiseworthy — meditate on these things. (Philippians 4:8)

Although the word *meditate* is often used today, it is considered more as the "absence of thought." In the passage above, it means the opposite. Paul said "meditate on" — or think seriously about — these things. In other words, focus on a peaceful spirit.

Focus on whatever is:

- *True* — that which will not let you down or vary with opinion; that which causes you to love truth.
- *Noble* — that which has the dignity of holiness upon it.
- *Just and pure* — that which is morally undefiled, meaning it is fit to be brought into the presence of God and used in His service.
- *Lovely* — that which calls forth love, encouragement, health, and well-being.
- *Of good report* — that which is positive and beneficial for man and God to hear.
- *If there is any virtue* — that which is of moral excellence, such as mercy and truth.

Think consistently on these things and build your life upon them.

This week, use Philippians 4:8-9 as you pray, asking the Lord to focus your thoughts and heart on these characteristics daily, that He might develop a favored spirit within you.

> **CONSIDER THIS:** Why are we ready to settle for outward appearance when we've been told that our hearts are of great value to the One we love and long to please? Ask yourself:
>
> - Is showing mercy something I actively and prayerfully strive to accomplish? Do I work toward this, practice this, and pray consistently for the gift of mercy in my life?
> - Do I build my life on absolute truth or on perceived truth? Do I base my life on the opinions of the culture or on circumstances?
> - Am I at peace with my choices and decisions and the ways I use my time and energy?

Process of Presentation

Mary was called "blessed," one whom the Lord chose, but it was her presentation of herself as a living sacrifice that allowed her to be a quiet influence for all generations. The announcement of the angel Gabriel was wondrous and God choosing Mary was a great honor, but she still had to say yes to the adventure before her. To understand how great Mary's sacrifice was, let's examine the whole picture:

- There was a possibility she could be stoned as an outcast.
- Her life would be one of mercy and truth as long as she lived.
- There would be no room for complaining, indiscretions, bad habits, convenient choices, or being absorbed into the culture.
- She would often be alone in her walk, and it would not be an easy one.

- She would raise, and then release, a Son whose tragic and painful death was foretold.

One thing we can be sure of is that Mary knew the Scriptures. She knew them well, and they were the basis of truth in her life. In fact, the knowledge of God's Word that she learned in the synagogue as the scrolls were read and her absolute faith in those words and God Himself allowed her to turn fear and doubt into joyful surrender.

Influence Begins with Understanding and Surrender

Luke 1:28-29 tells us that Mary was "troubled" when the angel addressed her as "blessed" and "highly favored one." After all, she was young and from humble surroundings, and these rather lofty terms seemed difficult to accept. *Troubled* here is a translation of the Greek word *diatarasso*, unique in the New Testament to this one verse. After all, this is the only time such an announcement was made. It is translated as "extreme agitation."

Luke 1:32-34 shows us that the fear Mary felt turned to doubt when the angel pronounced that she would give birth to "the Son of the Highest." She asked a logical question, "How can this be?" The Lord does not mind us asking questions or wanting to be sure that we thoroughly understand what He is asking us to do. However, once we get the answers, will we do as Mary did and surrender to His will?

Mary exchanged her fear and doubt for truth and facts of the absolute. She focused on God's care and love for her: "For I know the thoughts that I think toward you, says the LORD, thoughts of peace and not of evil, to give you a future and a hope" (Jeremiah 29:11).

Let's look at the facts together:

- The God of the Bible is on your side.
- He is compassionately concerned about you.
- You are on His mind and heart.

- He thinks good thoughts about you.
- His plans are peaceful and for your good.
- He has a unique future planned for you.
- God's plan for your future is a sure thing—an expected end, which is the actual definition of biblical hope.
- He wants you to have a peaceful life.

Peace in the Hebrew means "to be whole, sound, safe; to be completed, finished; to be at peace; to be in friendship with; to be made secure; prosperity." In John 14:27, Jesus said, "Peace I leave with you, My peace I give to you; not as the world gives do I give to you."

We Influence Others Through God's Word in Our Hearts

Imagine such a moment: You are fearful and perplexed, not sure of what to do or where to turn. Suddenly, the Word of God explodes in your heart and fills your mind as you remember, "The virgin shall conceive . . ." Mary had heard Isaiah 7:14 read in the temple. She remembered it, and suddenly she knew, *It's me!*

I am overcome with goose bumps just thinking about such a moment—to *know* God's good thoughts are with you and that you have been chosen as a living sacrifice because you *know* the Word of God.

Mary focused on presenting herself a living sacrifice in the final exchange of fear and doubt for absolute truth; she was able to genuinely reply, "Let it be to me according to your word" (Luke 1:38).

Result of Presentation

Luke 1:39 tells us that "Mary arose in those days and went into the hill country with haste." Once we surrender in the spirit of "Let it be to me according to your word," joy floods us, and we are energized to live a life of purpose. Fear and doubt are banished as surrender rises triumphantly. This is the life we were created for, the life that Jesus said He came to give us: "I have come that they may have life, and that they may have it more abundantly" (John 10:10).

Encouragement to Endure

It is noteworthy that the Lord, in His personal care for Mary, understood that she would need a human touch to walk through this supernatural announcement. He prepared Elizabeth, her cousin, to encourage her. Mary ran to the home of Elizabeth, just as the angel had instructed her to do, and she was greeted with joy:

> It happened, when Elizabeth heard the greeting of Mary, that the babe leaped in her womb; and Elizabeth was filled with the Holy Spirit. Then she spoke out with a loud voice and said, "Blessed are you among women, and blessed is the fruit of your womb!" (Luke 1:41-42)

When we present ourselves as living sacrifices, the Lord rushes in to give us the encouragement, strength, and joy we need to complete the task.

CONSIDER THIS: Can you think of someone the Lord sent into your life as an Elizabeth just at the time you needed him or her? Is there someone He might be calling you to encourage today?

Perhaps as you present yourself to Him, He will call you to be the Elizabeth in someone else's life. She is truly a character we can aspire to emulate: a godly woman, standing spiritually, ready to recognize God's work, regardless of how others may perceive it or even the sheer impossibility of the call.

Abide in the Profitable Scripture

The word *abide* speaks of holding fast, remaining steadfast and immovable. "If you abide in Me, and My words abide in you, you will ask what you desire, and it shall be done for you" (John 15:7).

Abiding in God's Word leads to a life of enduring faith. Joseph and Mary made the trip to Bethlehem, and Mary gave birth to Jesus. Soon after, they made the hasty and somewhat dangerous trip to Egypt. Finally, she returned to Nazareth with the hope of peace and a normal life, but it was not so. Jesus left the security of her home and began to travel without a place to lay His head, sharing a message that few understood. "Jesus said . . . 'Foxes have holes and birds of the air have nests, but the Son of Man has nowhere to lay His head'" (Matthew 8:20).

Mary saw the crowds surround Him with enthusiasm and then watched as they betrayed Him. Her own children thought Jesus was mad and urged her to stop Him. She tried to understand, but it was more than she could wrap her mind around. Instead, she remembered His promises and endured with faith.

Before it was written, Mary knew: He is "the God of patience and comfort" (Romans 15:5). The Greek word for *patience* here is *hupomone*. This patience is about strength. It is

> not the ability to sit down and bear things, but the ability to rise up and conquer them. God is He Who gives us the power to use any experience to lend greatness and glory to life. God is He in whom we learn to use joy and failure, achievement and disappointment alike, to enrich and to ennoble life, to make us more useful to others and to bring us nearer to Himself.[3]

Hupomone is the quality of God's character in us that does not allow surrender to circumstances but maintains an enduring, consistent faith. The writer of Hebrews said, "Cast not away therefore your confidence, which hath great recompence of reward. For ye have need of patience [*hupomone*], that, after ye have done the will of God, ye might receive the promise" (10:35-36, KJV).

Through Scripture memory, prayer, focusing on thoughts of truth and mercy, and journaling our praise, we can continue to be women of influence even as challenges, problems, and discouragements come into our lives. We display strength through the power of His Word hidden in our hearts.

CONSIDER THIS: When we respond with *hupomone*, the Holy Spirit begins forming the very nature and attributes of Christ in us. Is a life of consistent, enduring faith actually possible? Can we achieve this? If so, how?

She Finished Well

Mary stayed at the cross, watching Jesus' agony but still believing. With every painful gasp of breath He took, she suffered in anguish. It was the worst day of her life. How could she stay and watch such a thing? Surely she went back to His words that she had heard over and over: "Don't let this throw you. You trust God, don't you? Trust me" (John 14:1, MSG).

It was the truth, the absolute truth of her own Son, the words of God, that gave her the courage to stand by Him and endure onward to the cross. Mary had always known this day would come. She relived the prophecies and His teachings and remembered hope. Surely He would rise just as He'd said He would. "For as Jonah was three days and three nights in the belly of a huge fish, so the Son of Man will be three days and three nights in the heart of the earth" (Matthew 12:40, NIV).

Knowing the Word also assured her that the worst day of her life would be the best day for the world. There would be new opportunities, new mercy, new hope for all generations, and this allowed her to continue presenting herself to the will of God.

Once again, she faced her fears, focused on absolute truth, and surrendered in belief. She finally understood that Jesus had not come to make life better for the Jews, as many had hoped. Instead, He came to make lives *new*. With *hupomone* (patience), she waited at the cross for the hope that would surely come.

She Knew the Heart of God

Through every phase of her journey, Mary went back to the Scriptures she learned in the synagogue and from her family. They taught of a personal Yahweh, the one true and living God who was faithful. When we find ourselves unsure or fearful of the future, we can go back to the heart of God as shown in His Word and find great comfort and strength. Perhaps Mary remembered these words of Isaiah as he described the everlasting God:

> Have you not known?
> Have you not heard?
> The everlasting God, the LORD,
> The Creator of the ends of the earth,
> Neither faints nor is weary.
> His understanding is unsearchable.
> He gives power to the weak,
> And to those who have no might He increases strength. . . .
> But those who wait on the LORD
> Shall renew their strength;
> They shall mount up with wings like eagles,
> They shall run and not be weary,
> They shall walk and not faint. (40:28-29,31)

Isaiah first explained **who God is** (verse 28):
- *The everlasting God* — He transcends all time.
- *The Creator of the ends of the earth* — His power reaches beyond where man is able to exist, even to the "ends" of the earth.

- *He neither faints nor is weary*—His source of power is incredible and unending.

He then explained **what He offers us** (verse 29):
- Power to the weak
- Endurance for weariness

Lastly, he explained **what we must do** (verse 31). Those who wait on the Lord are those who:
- Expect Him to come through
- Have confidence, as a child in a parent
- Believe God will manifest Himself in a given situation
- Know He is worth the wait

As Roy Hession said in his book *The Calvary Road*, you, like Mary, will know "whatever may be our experience of failure and barrenness, He is never defeated, His power is boundless!"[4] He has risen indeed, and He reigns at the right hand of the Father. Amen. In heaven, they are always praising Him for His victory.

CONSIDER THIS: What causes people to give up on their faith and convictions?

Disappointment	Difficult Circumstances
Illness	Financial Pressure
Family Conflict	Overwhelming Stress
Global Problems (war, AIDS, famine, pestilence, etc.)	Other

Fear played a big part of Mary's decision to present herself to the will of God. When Mary felt afraid, she didn't let that overwhelm her. She clung to the truth of God's words and surrendered to His will.

DISCUSS: How much power does fear and facing the unknown have in our choice to surrender to the will of God? Is your life ruled by facts (absolute truth) or feelings and opinions? When you fear something, is it a lack of confidence in God or yourself?

Do you sometimes feel powerless to endure? Do you know Christians who were once vocal and strong in their faith but have given up on loving and serving God? Give examples of what things might lead to a lack of endurance in the life of a believer.

Diane's Rules for Overcoming Fear

- Don't give in to fear; hope is around the corner.
- Base your vision for any action steps on faith and truth rather than opinion and gossip.
- Believe in God's will for you — that is, that He wants the best for your life.
- Depend on God's resources and abilities rather than your own.
- Replace fear with a declaration of genuine, personal faith in God.
- Don't settle for the natural when you have the supernatural.
- Let your first word always be your best word.

Chapter 3

Monica, the Mother of Saint Augustine

Persevering Prayer

by Donna Gaines

Culture and Background

AD 333–387[1]

The society Monica lived in was dominated by Roman customs and culture. Marriages were arranged, and Roman law stated that a woman officially became a matron of marriageable age at twelve years old, though the average age a woman got married was fourteen. A woman would then leave her family and take up residence with her husband's family. Domestic abuse and marital infidelity by husbands was common at the time, and a woman was virtually powerless in such a situation, though divorce was allowed in Roman society.

Only men could hold political office and enjoy a formal education. Some women were educated informally in their homes, but this was seen as a way to increase their value as wives. A woman had few political rights, and her place was in the home taking care of her children. In the fourth century, upper-class Roman women began to experience more financial freedom through changes in inheritance laws. However, Monica was not among this class.[2]

Christianity had an impact on the status of women. During times of persecution in the first three centuries after Christ, women had proven their devotion by being willing to die for their faith. In some cases, such as the witness of Perpetua, women had shown themselves to be truer in the face of death than some men. Women were praised for the stands they took for Christ.

Christians had experienced religious toleration ever since the time of Constantine and the Edict of Milan in AD 313. In AD 380, Christianity became the state religion of the Roman Empire through an edict issued by Theodosius I.[3] During the time that Monica lived, Christians were no longer dying the martyr's death because of these imperial reforms, and asceticism or monasticism became a popular way to show devotion to Christ.

A Christian woman distinguished herself either in devotion to her husband and children or by adopting the ascetic lifestyle. A few noble women began having Bible studies in their homes for other women and in a few cases acted as patronesses to popular Christian preachers or bishops. However, other women were not afforded this kind of opportunity because the responsibilities of their home and family would not allow this luxury of fellowship.[4]

Nothing grips at the heart of a mother as much as a wayward child. She awakens every morning with a heavy heart, and she falls asleep at night on a pillow wet from her tears. Such was the despair of Monica, the mother of Augustine. Grieved by his rebellion and open sin, Monica cried out to God for the conversion of her son. Turning to an unnamed bishop and pleading for advice, she received these words of wisdom: "Go your way; as you live, it cannot be that the son of these tears should perish."[5] These words were used by the Lord to console her anguish and encourage her not to give up as she prayed nine more years for the conversion of her son. Little did she know, God would not only answer her prayers for Augustine's salvation, but also this son of her travail would become the greatest of the early church fathers, a man whose life continues to impact the church today.

Augustine, a brilliant theologian and philosopher, openly wrote of his reprobate life as a young man. He credits his mother, Monica, as the catalyst of his salvation. Through her earnest prayers for his soul, her unconditional love, and her consistent life of faith, he was converted.

Mother, Your faithful one, wept to You on my behalf more than most mothers weep after the bodily deaths of their children. For by the light of faith and the Spirit she received from You, she saw that I was dead. You heard her, O Lord, and did not reject her tears as they poured down and watered the earth under her wherever she prayed. Yes, Lord, You truly did heed her prayers.[6]

Monica was born in Tagaste, North Africa, in AD 333 to Christian parents. She married at an early age; her husband, Patritius, was a pagan man with a violent temper and lax morals. They had three children: Augustine, the eldest; Navigius, the second eldest; and a daughter, Perpetua. Monica's gentle and quiet spirit eventually led to the salvation of her husband (in AD 371), who died shortly after being accepted into the church.

Monica chose not to remarry. She devoted herself to praying for her son and eventually followed him to Milan. "There the one wish of her life was met. Augustine was converted in 386, and was baptized by Ambrose, Easter (April 25), 387."[7]

Prayer as Presentation

There are many things we don't understand about prayer, but if you have studied the Bible, you realize that prayer is important and that God answers the prayers of His children. We are told in Romans 12:1, "Present your bodies a living and holy sacrifice, acceptable to God, which is your spiritual service of worship" (NASB). We present our bodies to God through prayer. As we offer ourselves to God, He moves and answers on our behalf.

Prayer Is Relationship

As Jennifer Kennedy Dean stated in her book *Heart's Cry*, "Prayer is not an activity, but a relationship. . . . It is not the cry of the lips, but the cry of the heart that God hears."[8] It is obvious that Monica cried out to God, not only with her lips but also with her heart.

Monica had developed such a sweet intimacy with the Lord that she trusted Him with all of her relationships. She trusted even when her husband was disobedient to the Word. She chose to turn to the Lord and live a life of purposeful devotion to Christ. She did not allow her husband's disobedience to defeat her; instead, it strengthened her resolve to pray and trust the Lord. Her relationship with Christ eventually brought her mother-in-law as well as her husband to Christ.

Prayer is the power source for living. It is to our spiritual lives what breathing is to our physical lives. E. M. Bounds, who took seriously the command to "pray without ceasing," said, "Prayer is the mainspring of life. We pray as we live; we live as we pray. Life will never be finer than the quality of the prayer closet."[9]

CONSIDER THIS: Do you experience intimacy with the Lord? Are you able to trust Him with the relationships that are most dear to you? How would you rate your prayer life? Do you know God well enough to trust Him completely? What can you do to improve your relationship with Christ?

Learn to Listen

Many times in Scripture, Jesus said, "He who has ears to hear, let him hear!"[10] He also said in John 10 that His sheep hear and know His voice. You learn to discern someone's voice by spending time with him or her. The best ways to spend time with the Lord and learn to hear His voice are through reading His Word and praying.

Monica poured her heart out to the Lord with tears and great persistence, but she also learned to listen. Not only did the bishop encourage her with assurance that God would answer her prayers, but the Lord also granted her a dream that Augustine described in his book *Confessions*. In this dream, a young man assured her that the son for whom she was lamenting would one day be where she was as well.

If we will listen for the Lord, He will answer us when we cry out. Many times in my own life, the Lord has used a verse from Scripture to soothe my soul or answer the cry of my heart. So often, that verse will be confirmed over and over again.

Systematically reading through the Bible every year and keeping a prayer journal are two disciplines that pay rich dividends. It is here that the Lord will meet with you, just as He met with His faithful ones in His Word. I recommend that you have a special place and time that you meet with the Lord on a daily basis. This time with Him needs to be treated as an appointment and guarded as the most important part of your day.

I personally use *The One Year Bible*. This Bible is divided into 365 daily readings, with each day including a portion from the Old Testament, New Testament, Psalms, and Proverbs. It takes about fifteen minutes at the most to read an entry each day. (I also recommend *The One Year Chronological Bible*.) Listen to God when you read. Expect to encounter Him in His living Word, and then spend time in prayer. Record your requests and always record His answers. What a boost to your faith as you look back at God's answers to your prayers.

When Moses was given the instructions for the tabernacle, God told him, "There I will meet with you; and from above the mercy seat, from between the two cherubim which are upon the ark of the testimony, I will speak to you about all that I will give you in commandment for the sons of Israel" (Exodus 25:22, NASB). The priests ministered in the tabernacle because the presence of the Lord was there. God spoke to them once a year on the Day of Atonement.

A. W. Tozer, whom many called "a twentieth-century prophet" even in his own lifetime, said,

This Flame of the Presence was the beating heart of the Levitical order. Without it all the appointments of the tabernacle were characters of some unknown language, having no meaning for Israel or for us. The greatest fact of the tabernacle was that Jehovah was there; a Presence was waiting within the veil.[11]

Jesus Christ has made the way for us to enjoy the perpetual presence of the Lord in our lives. The Bible tells us that we are living temples of God. Instead of residing in the Holy of Holies of the tabernacle, He now resides within us. Hebrews 4:16 says, "Let us therefore come boldly to the throne of grace, that we may obtain mercy and find grace to help in time of need." We don't have to wait for Sunday or a special day of the year; we have the blessed privilege of meeting with Him and experiencing His presence every day.

CONSIDER THIS: Do you have a special place and time that you meet with the Lord? Are you systematically reading through His Word each day? Where and what time would be best for your appointment with the Lord? How will you prepare the place where you meet with Him? How often are you aware of His perpetual presence?

Learn to Long for Him

When I was pregnant with our third child, I began crying out to the Lord to know Him more intimately. Since there is nothing more powerful than praying the Word of God, I began to pray Psalm 42:1: "As the deer pants for the water brooks, so pants my soul for You, O God." I asked the Lord to make this longing a reality in my life. I realized after about six months that I couldn't put my Bible down. I was learning so much and hearing the voice of my Savior through His Word. I was so excited that I wanted to share what I was learning with everyone.

This kind of hunger is awakened by the Lord, but we must pursue it. A. W. Tozer said, "Complacency is a deadly foe of all spiritual growth.

Acute desire must be present or there will be no manifestation of Christ to His people. He waits to be wanted. Too bad that with many of us He waits so long, so very long, in vain."[12]

If we will faithfully pursue Christ through prayer and His Word, we will find that He Himself becomes our great reward. We no longer seek the blessings of His hand—we seek His face. At the end of her life, Monica was satisfied to die and be buried anywhere the Lord willed. God had answered her prayers, and she trusted Him with everything—life and death. In her book *Live a Praying Life*, Jennifer Kennedy Dean said,

It is during the process of prayer that the praying person is brought to total submission to the Father. During the process of prayer, God weans our hearts from the things we so want and fastens them on Him. We start the process desiring something from Him and end it desiring only Him.[13]

CONSIDER THIS: In John 15:7-8, Jesus said, "If you abide in Me, and My Words abide in you, ask whatever you wish, and it will be done for you. My Father is glorified *by this*, that you bear much fruit, and so prove to be My disciples" (NASB, emphasis added). What does "by this" refer to? Are you abiding in God's Word? When was the last time you experienced an answer to prayer? When was the last time you sensed the Lord speaking to you through a particular verse of Scripture? What was the verse?

Learn to Persevere

Jesus told a parable in Luke 18 about a persistent woman and an unrighteous judge. In this parable, a widow comes to the judge repeatedly requesting justice against someone who has harmed her. This unrighteous man grants her justice because she is wearing him out with her requests. Jesus told us to learn a lesson from this evil judge:

Even he rendered a just decision in the end. So don't you think
God will surely give justice to his chosen people who cry out
to him day and night? Will he keep putting them off? I tell
you, he will grant justice to them quickly! But when the Son of
Man returns, how many will he find on earth who have faith?
(verses 7-8, NLT)

It is obvious that the Lord is comparing persistence with faith. If
we really believe that the Lord will answer our requests, we will not
cease asking until we are assured of an answer. Could it be that we
are apathetic and lack perseverance because of our lack of faith? In
Matthew 7:7-8, we are told to ask and keep on asking, to seek and keep
on seeking, to knock and keep on knocking. The Lord added in verse
11, "If you sinful people know how to give good gifts to your children,
how much more will your heavenly Father give good gifts to those who
ask him" (NLT).

Has there ever been a time in your life when you had to persevere in prayer? Let's face it: Persevering in prayer is difficult—it is war.
Ephesians 6:18 wraps up the description of the full armor of God that
we have been given for battle: "With all prayer and petition pray at all
times in the Spirit, and with this in view, be on the alert with all perseverance and petition for all the saints" (NASB). We have been given the
Spirit of God to empower us and the weapons of warfare to protect us.
We are to stand against the Enemy with the Word of God—the sword
of the Spirit—and prayer.

You may be asking, "But how do I do this?" Let me share with
you one example of a time when we entered into persevering prayer
for our son. When he was in high school, he went through a period of
rebellion. He was doing things he shouldn't have been doing, and the
Lord was blowing his cover every time. We grounded him for about six
months. I was so frustrated because I knew he belonged to the Lord
and that he knew so much more than he was living.

The Lord, in His grace, allowed me to attend a luncheon where

I was seated across the table from Karolyn Chapman, the wife of Dr. Gary Chapman (author of *The Five Love Languages* and several other books). I don't remember how the topic of rebellious children came up at the table, but Carolyn shared about her own son who had gone through a period of rebellion. I asked her how she had dealt with it. She said that she had enlisted a group of prayer warriors for her son. She said to ask only those who you know really understand how to intercede. She suggested sharing with them what is happening and keeping them updated on what the Lord is doing.

I couldn't wait to get home and follow her advice. My husband and I prayed about who we would ask to join us in prayer for our son. Each person we requested to join us in prayer was more than willing. Through a series of events, the Lord broke through, and our son came to his father one night and confessed his sin, wanting to be right with the Lord and with us. My husband phoned these prayer warriors, and each one came to our home that evening. We had such a sweet time of prayer with our son, and his life has not been the same since.

Perhaps you are facing a difficult trial in your marriage, job, or some other situation in your life. I encourage you to memorize and meditate on the Word of God. God will meet you in His Word, and you will receive counsel and comfort. Take Him at His Word. Pray His Word back to Him. Maybe you are facing a difficult time right now. You may feel as though you are having trouble keeping your head above water. Could it be that, like Peter when he stepped out of the boat, you have your eyes on the storm and not the Savior? Take time to write out the verses the Lord uses to encourage you. Read them, memorize them, and meditate on them. It is the power of God's Spirit, His Word, and prayer that will bring you through.

Persistent prayer is fervent, and it is often accompanied by tears. Remember the cry of Hannah in the Old Testament? She cried out to God for a son. She poured out her heart with tears but no words. The Lord heard the cry of her heart and answered her prayers (see 1 Samuel 1). Bill Gothard said in his book *The Power of Crying Out*, "Though

Hannah's physical voice was silent, God heard her fervent, poured-out prayer in that place and granted her a son. Little Samuel grew up to become one of the Lord's most dedicated servants—and a mighty prayer warrior himself."[14]

CONSIDER THIS: What specific thing is God using in your life to call you to persevere in prayer? Is your lack of faith keeping you from persevering? Have you allowed yourself to become apathetic?

Leaving a Legacy

The Lord rewarded Monica's persevering prayer. Her son was saved and became one of the greatest theologians the world has known. Her faithful walk with the Lord and her intimacy in prayer challenged her son to follow Christ with the same fervency he had witnessed in his mother. Are you passing on a passion for Christ to your children and grandchildren? What about as an older woman to the next generation?

God has chosen the instrument of prayer to move and accomplish His will. The Bible tells us in Revelation 5:8 that our prayers are held in golden bowls before the throne of God and rise before Him as incense. These verses let us know that our prayers are tangible in heaven. Are you presenting yourself before His throne in prayer? Are you investing in eternity? Choose to pass on a legacy of faith to the next generation. Pray in such a way that those around you will ask you the same thing Jesus' disciples asked Him: "Teach us to pray!" (Luke 11:1).

God shapes the world by prayer. Prayers are deathless.
They outlive the lives of those who uttered them.

— E. M. Bounds

DISCUSS: What causes people to give up on prayer? How can you develop your prayer life to the point that God can entrust you to stand in the gap to see His will brought from heaven to earth? What will you do, beginning today, to enhance your ability to hear His voice? Your longing for Him? Your own perseverance in prayer?

Chapter 4

Sarah Edwards

Hospitality and Encouragement

by Lisa Young

Culture and Background

1710–1758

Life in colonial New England was a time of political uncertainty and imminent war. However, the settlers worked hard and created an essentially middle-class society with almost no poverty. The churches were no longer persecuted sects seeking religious freedom; they were established churches that influenced culture.

Puritans celebrated and honored marriage. Because America was still such a young nation, it needed the stability of the family. More than 75 percent of the population married, and widows and widowers were encouraged to remarry. The average age when a woman married was twenty-three. Wives were well protected in this new society. For example, a man could be punished for speaking harsh words to his wife.[1]

Medicine was still somewhat experimental, and infant mortality was high. The primary education for children in colonial days included reading, writing, simple math, poems, and prayers. The three most commonly used books were the Bible, a primer, and a hornbook. While boys studied more advanced, academic subjects, the girls learned to assume the duties of a wife and mother.

Many women in the early 1700s owned no more than two to four hand-sewn, wool outfits. Clothing was not washed very often, and in some cases, a piece of clothing that did not directly touch the skin might never be washed.[2] Some of the daily tasks for a wife and mother included making clothing, gathering firewood, cooking, growing and preserving produce, cleaning the house, and feeding livestock — and this only touches the surface.[3]

The hospitality of Sarah Edwards changed the lives of many young men who studied with her husband, Jonathan. It was said that "her sweet and winning manners and ready conversation" made fast acquaintances with the visitors; they felt as if they were "home."[4] With modest means and eleven children to care for, she spared no effort to welcome guests and provide for their convenience and comfort. The time she spent praying and offering words of encouragement was powerful enough to send visitors away changed. Sarah Edwards influenced her generation through the gift of hospitality.

When you hear the word *hospitality*, what is the first thing that pops into your mind? Being from the Deep South, the first things that come to my mind are entertaining and great food as well as some of the ever-popular entertainment icons: Paula Dean, Rachael Ray, or Martha Stewart; their delicious meals with eye-catching presentations certainly put them in a class of their own when it comes to entertaining.

So often our definition of hospitality is formed from the cultural leanings of our time. We associate hospitality with mere qualities of entertaining, hosting parties, and serving food. Could this picture of hospitality fall short of what God intended it to be? Could it be that God has something deeper and richer to say about hospitality?

There is great comfort in knowing that whatever our human understanding might be, God expands it to a new, dynamic level. Because

God increases our ability to understand and apply lessons we learn from others, we can look at a true icon of hospitality: Sarah Edwards, the eighteenth-century wife of an energetic pastor and theologian. Sarah's life presents the biblical perspective of what hospitality should be in each of our lives. Her life demonstrates that God can take hold of an ordinary woman and use her to do extraordinary things for the world.

CONSIDER THIS: Think of the challenges you might be facing that keep you from being a woman of hospitality and encouragement. Compare them to those of Sarah Edwards:

- She was married at a young age to an outspoken evangelist.
- She bore eleven children and raised them without luxury.
- She watched her husband focus intently on Scripture and teaching while she carried the responsibilities of the home and child rearing.
- She provided an atmosphere at home that stirred strangers to cross the doorstep anticipating replenishment of the deepest kind.

This is the life that an ordinary woman lived, one that she embraced fully by the strength afforded through an intimate relationship with God. This same strength is available to us. The same impact Sarah had on others is possible for you and me.

Sarah Edwards may have lived in the eighteenth century, but her life had strong effects on people throughout the years, into the twenty-first century and beyond. A look at her legacy gives us insight into how God uses kindness, compassion, and knowledge of His Word to strengthen generations and change lives. Throughout the tapestry of Sarah's life, we see hospitality as the thread that allowed the extension of God's grace to be shared with others.

The Thread of Hospitality

The word *hospitality* comes from the Latin root *hospes* and the Greek *hostis*. The meaning of each of these terms is significant. We get the word *hospital* from *hospes*, which seems fitting since a hospital is a place where people in need of physical attention can be cared for.

The Greek root *hostis* has a very different connotation and application. The original meaning was "stranger" or "enemy." In early American history, villages were located far apart, and there was no means of communication except by word of mouth. When a stranger approached a home or village, he or she would be viewed and treated as an enemy until it was determined that the person posed no threat. At that point, the stranger would be welcomed and offered food, lodging, and fellowship with someone in the community. The person was invited to share the community experience; thus, the stranger was shown hospitality.

In the early church, several symbols were used to represent the idea of hospitality to greet fellow believers. It is likely that the popular fish symbol was adopted by the leaders of the early church as a greeting. Jesus referenced fishing on many occasions and used fish to feed the multitudes. It is a symbol with which His followers could easily identify. During the critical time of persecution in the early church, in order to determine if they were encountering a fellow follower of Christ, Christians would draw the first half of a fish in the sand. Then the other individual would complete the fish to show a joint commitment to the cause of Christ.[5]

As another symbol of hospitality, Paul instructed the early church to greet one another with a "holy kiss," signifying the welcoming of believers to their region of ministry.[6] Often, those in the early church would travel great lengths and endure trying circumstances in order to be with other Christians. Perhaps Paul wanted the early church to realize the importance of giving a sincere welcome to its fellow strugglers with this more intimate gesture.

If we fast-forward to the fifteenth century, we find Christopher Columbus and his men sailing on behalf of the queen of Spain to find new lands. When they finally reached land on their second journey, they came ashore on the island of Guadeloupe and were greeted by the inhabitants of the island. Surely there was a moment of fear and uncertainty as the natives approached the group. However, history tells us that the men were greeted with kindness and were given pineapples to show that they were welcome on the island. Columbus then returned to Europe with pineapples and pineapple plants, illustrating the hospitality extended to the crew.[7]

The pineapple became the symbol for hospitality and was carried to the American colonies by the European inhabitants. Often, a pineapple was used in architecture of the new communities to show a hospitable atmosphere. Thus, to this day, in some homes you will find this same use of the pineapple to commemorate the history of hospitality among the people.

CONSIDER THIS: What experiences from your past have influenced your concept of hospitality (family traditions, friendships, travel)? Do you see hospitality as something reserved for those who have a knack for entertaining and a passion for good food? If so, how do you measure up to that standard?

Ask God to help you embrace His view of hospitality. It can serve as a powerful testimony in your life and the lives of those around you.

The Depth of Hospitality

Despite these examples throughout history, hospitality holds a limited definition of dinner parties or overnight stays for many people. In order to understand the depth of hospitality, we must move beyond our preconceived notions.

Let's travel beyond the pages of a dictionary, where the writers underscore our limitations, and instead discover what the Bible has to say. By searching Scripture and looking at the model that Jesus provided, we can accurately paint a portrait of this life-changing quality.

John 4 gives us a beautiful snapshot of Jesus' encounter with a woman who was in desperate need of hospitality. In this passage, we see the true definition of hospitality and the depth it can bring to each of us.

Based on John 4, I offer this three-pronged definition of *hospitality*:

- Hospitality is extending grace to someone in need.
- Hospitality is kindness packaged with purpose.
- Hospitality is graciousness extended from the heart.

Jesus was traveling to Galilee, a journey on which He could have chosen several routes. Yet He chose a direction that led Him and the disciples directly through Samaria, an area that was avoided by Jews because the Samaritans were a despised race.

> So he left Judea and returned to Galilee. He had to go through Samaria on the way. Eventually he came to the Samaritan village of Sychar, near the field that Jacob gave to his son Joseph. Jacob's well was there; and Jesus, tired from the long walk, sat wearily beside the well about noontime. (John 4:3-6, NLT)

The phrase "had to" leads us to believe that Jesus had no other choice. Perhaps it wasn't about choice as much as divine appointment.

Often, God leads us down a path because there is something significant He wants us to experience. If we could see beyond our understanding of the road we are traveling—be it a hardship in a career, an illness, or a broken relationship—we could grab hold of encounters that God has appointed for His will to be done in our lives. Solomon offered a great encouragement in Proverbs 3:5-6: "Trust in the LORD with all your heart and lean not on your own understanding; in all your ways acknowledge him, and he will make your paths straight" (NIV).

Hospitality is about opportunity, and opportunity is often found in unlikely places and along unlikely paths. John 4:6 tells us that Jesus was tired and sat by the well. It is always encouraging for me to see the humanity of Christ in Scripture; it shows me that I have a Savior who can identify with where I have been. He had been traveling on some tough terrain and needed a break.

Soon a Samaritan woman came to draw water, and Jesus said to her, "Please give me a drink." He was alone at the time because his disciples had gone into the village to buy some food.

The woman was surprised, for Jews refuse to have anything to do with Samaritans. She said to Jesus, "You are a Jew, and I am a Samaritan woman. Why are you asking me for a drink?" (verses 7-9, NLT)

Jesus broke many barriers in offering hospitality to the Samaritan woman despite the potential repercussions and backlash. He crossed the lines of race, gender, and religion in order to meet her needs. He extended grace to her. And although Jesus was the one asking for a drink, He offered true hospitality by engaging her in conversation.

The woman questioned Him about His request, and He responded with a statement that changed everything she had believed up until this moment: "If you only knew the gift God has for you and who you are speaking to, you would ask me, and I would give you living water" (verse 10, NLT).

Hospitality is ultimately about helping others understand the gift God has for them. That gift, God's grace, is the component of hospitality that brings depth and richness. It might be shared over a drink of water or casual meal or through an overnight stay in your home. But no matter what act it is cloaked in, hospitality is more than fulfilling a role as a hostess; it is all about answering the call to reveal and share God's grace with others.

The Effects of Hospitality

In this story in John 4, we see that Jesus had no reservations about telling the Samaritan woman who He was. He wanted to reveal His grace and mercy to her. He also had no qualms about revealing the truth of who she was.

Through the exchange of words by the well, Jesus led this woman to see who she really was. She had already admitted that she was a Samaritan. That alone said something. She knew that her community and her people were considered "less than" in terms of character and status. But Jesus' words helped her to understand her personal condition, not just her social standing.

It isn't difficult to accept our position in life as a group because there is comfort in numbers. But when we get down to personal accountability, we have a much more difficult time facing the truth. When we are on our own, we feel isolated and vulnerable. Jesus singled out this woman as their conversation continued:

"Go and get your husband," Jesus told her.

"I don't have a husband," the woman replied.

Jesus said, "You're right! You don't have a husband — for you have had five husbands, and you aren't even married to the man you're living with now. You certainly spoke the truth!"

"Sir," the woman said, "you must be a prophet." (verses 16-19, NLT)

At this point she realized she had many deeper flaws than simply being a Samaritan woman. Jesus' words revealed her sinful condition. Seeing the truth of her condition brought conviction and, ultimately, conversion.

Jesus' willingness to show hospitality provided Him a platform to share with this woman not only her condition but also the good news of who He is. That led her to turn from her old life and begin a new journey with Him. Convicted of her sin, she allowed Jesus to change her that day. She left the well knowing that Jesus was no ordinary man. But she couldn't keep the news to herself. "Many of the Samaritans from that town believed in him because of the woman's testimony" (John 4:39, NIV). Jesus changed her world, and she became a world-changer.

CONSIDER THIS: None of us likes to come face-to-face with our flaws. It's much easier to point out other people's flaws than to reflect on our own. But we will not experience change nor will we be able to help bring about change in others if we don't deal first with our sin. Ask Jesus to point out the sin in your life right now. Accept the truth about your condition. Use that conviction to experience conversion (change).

In my daily time with the Lord, I follow this process so that change can occur in my life. Make it a daily practice in your own life, and you'll begin to see God change you from the inside out.

The Call of Hospitality

I'm thankful for the exposure to hospitality that my family gave me growing up. As I mentioned, I was raised in the South. Southerners are known for southern hospitality. However, my parents demonstrated the deeper hospitality modeled by Jesus.

Through dinner parties with family and friends, great meals on the patio picnic tables, and church guests staying overnight, I saw hospitality in the real world. Our home was known for its generosity in serving meals and hosting guests. We didn't have a lavish home; in fact, it was quite the opposite. That wasn't what mattered. The heart of the environment created a venue for hospitality. Those who came through the doors of our home came from all walks of life and had various needs. They were welcomed not because of what we had to offer but because of what Jesus had offered us.

> In his grace, God has given us different gifts for doing certain things well. . . . Love each other with genuine affection, and take delight in honoring each other. Never be lazy, but work hard and serve the Lord enthusiastically. . . . When God's people are in need, be ready to help them. Always be eager to practice hospitality. (Romans 12:6,10-11,13, NLT)

We who have received the grace of our Lord Jesus should "always be eager to practice hospitality." That means we should look for opportunities to extend grace to someone in need, share kindness packaged with a purpose, and reflect graciousness from the heart.

This was Sarah Edwards' strength. Her home was not a palace of perfection but a place of protection for all who entered. It is easy to bring up the challenges that Sarah faced as she raised her children and supported her minister husband in rural Connecticut, yet she faced them with the grace that she received from her relationship with God. Because of her strong faith and the realization of God's grace, she was enormously gifted in extending hospitality to her family and friends as well as strangers.

Her husband was perhaps the biggest recipient of Sarah's hospitality. This may seem unusual to consider, but the reality is that our spouses need hospitality. They need to be welcomed into the home and shown grace in many situations. Many times Jonathan Edwards would return from travel and ministry endeavors with a wounded spirit and tired body. His replenishment often came through Sarah's love and grace. She brought recovery to her husband and ministered to him with the strength and power of God. Their union was reflective of mutual respect and generosity in meeting each other's needs.

We may think that giving generously of ourselves to our husbands is a small or insignificant thing, but that is a myth. It is exactly the opposite. Whenever I serve my husband and extend grace to him, our relationship deepens and the bond between us is strengthened. The hospitality I give to my husband is like no other available to him.

Hospitality also breeds greatness in our children. There is much talk these days about the next generation and what lies ahead for them. I am encouraged by the deposit of greatness that Sarah Edwards made in the lives of her children. They are shining examples of how an ordinary woman who is touched by the supernatural hospitality of God can impact future generations. When you look at the accomplishments of her family, you see what a legacy she built.

By 1900, less than two hundred years later, the marriage of John and Sarah Edwards had produced:

- Thirteen college presidents
- Sixty-five professors
- One hundred lawyers and a dean of an outstanding law school
- Thirty judges
- Sixty-six physicians and a dean of a medical school
- Eighty holders of public office, including:
  - Three U.S. senators
  - Three mayors of large cities
  - Three state governors
  - One U.S. vice president
  - One controller for the U.S. Treasury[8]

More Than a Mere Visit

Many travelers came through the Edwards's home, and Sarah was the primary hostess. The door was open to strangers and friends alike. Often, Sarah hosted fellow ministers who arrived exhausted and ill. She nursed their physical, emotional, and spiritual needs with hospitality.

Samuel Hopkins, famous author and renowned abolitionist, wrote of her, "She knew the heart of a stranger." He also recalled being

> received with great kindness by Mrs. Edwards. . . . I was very gloomy and most of the time retired in my chamber. After some days, Mrs. Edwards came . . . and said as I now [am] a member of the family for a season, she felt herself interested in my welfare. . . . I told her . . . I was in a Christ-less, grace-less state . . . upon which we entered into a free conversation and . . . she told me that she had prayed respecting me since I had been in the family; that she trusted I should receive life and comfort and doubted not that God intended yet to do great things by me.[9]

At the time, Sarah had seven small children, but her prayers and words of encouragement were powerful enough to send Hopkins on his way with strength and courage.

Sarah's display of hospitality is a tremendous example for each of us. It is a true reflection of God's words found in Scripture: "Live in harmony with each other. Don't be too proud to enjoy the company of ordinary people" (Romans 12:16, NLT). God gives us the opportunity to extend hospitality to everyone. We should never consider ourselves to be above sharing hospitality with anyone. Jesus modeled this with the Samaritan woman. She was an unlikely recipient of conversation with the King of Kings and Lord of Lords, yet He humbled Himself in order to give her much-needed grace.

CONSIDER THIS: God is calling each of us to use hospitality as a tool for extending grace. We have received grace from Him, and it should overflow into the lives of others. Pray that God will open your eyes to opportunities to extend His grace to others. Look for ways to be hospitable in everyday, common circumstances.

Also, identify the enemies of hospitality that lurk in your life. God wants each of us to become world-changers just like the Samaritan woman and Sarah Edwards. But Satan does his best to persuade us that we aren't capable of this; he tries to thwart God's work in our lives. He uses the weapons of fear, insecurity, and apathy to keep us from living lives of hospitality and meaning. We must be intentional to overcome these attacks.

Do you find yourself contemplating the following questions and thoughts?

FEAR:

- What are the things I fear the most when it comes to reaching out?
- Am I afraid that people will think I'm weird?
- Am I worried that my house isn't big enough or nice enough?

INSECURITY:

- What if I'm not smart enough, rich enough, or beautiful enough to give to someone?
- What if I'm just not capable?

APATHY:

- What difference does it make? I'm only one person.
- Hospitality is better left to someone else at some other time in some other place.

Satan uses these lies to keep you from discovering the extraordinary and full life that God wants for you. Don't fall for them. Remember, "The thief comes only to steal and kill and destroy; I have come that they may have life, and have it to the full" (John 10:10, NIV).

No matter who you are or where you live, you can reach out to people. When you reach one life, you reach one community. And when you reach one community, you can reach one nation and, ultimately, the world.

In many ways, hospitality is a rare commodity. But simple acts of kindness open the door for relationships, which lead to changed lives. Just as Christ has changed your world, you, too, can become a world-changer through hospitality.

Chapter 5

Lottie Moon

Consecration, Compassion, and Obedience

by Susie Hawkins

Culture and Background

1840–1912

The nineteenth century brought astounding changes to the world. Just a few of the prominent names of those who lived in this century communicate the advances to modern civilization, from science to political thought: Louis Pasteur, Madame Curie, Charles Darwin, Karl Marx, and Sigmund Freud. In addition, the Industrial Revolution brought the construction of railroads and steamships, providing more efficient transportation for people and commodities.

This century marked many changes for women as well. Until this time, women were not allowed to give evidence in court, nor did they have the right to speak in public before an audience.[1] When a woman married, her husband became the legal owner of her possessions and inheritance. But by the middle of the century, the women's movement had gained strength in America, resulting in a woman's right to own property and increased opportunities for education, travel, and business.

The church in this century saw the explosion of the modern missions era.

Men such as William Carey, David Livingstone, and Hudson Taylor ventured to faraway continents, bringing the light of the gospel to the indigenous people there. Their firsthand reports of these mysterious cultures and lands caught the interest of American Christians. Women in churches of all denominations began forming missions "societies" that collected funds to support missions efforts and raise awareness of missions needs. This new interest in foreign missions offered women unprecedented opportunities. It was in this atmosphere that Lottie Moon emerged.

Lottie Moon's affluent upbringing afforded her opportunities not widely available to women of the time. She received her master of arts, one of the first ever awarded to a woman by a southern institution, and was called "the most educated woman in the South" by John Broadus, a nineteenth-century Christian scholar and preacher.[2] However, there were very few opportunities for educated females in the mid-1800s, with the exception of teaching school.

When Lottie first sensed the call to missions, women were not allowed on the mission field except as wives of missionaries. Several years later, however, churches began to appoint single women to serve alongside missionary couples. It is easy to see that the unusual opportunities in education in her young life were part of God's plan to call her into a life of influence for generations.

From the short biography of Lottie Moon, we can identify three words that best describe the personal sacrifice she made by giving her life in response to God's call. A close study of these words should enhance our own understanding of what it means to be a woman who is willing to sacrifice everything to follow Christ.

Consecration: Body and Soul

In the pages of her Bible, Lottie Moon left behind a self-portrait of her heart as she wrote, "O, that I could consecrate myself, soul and body, to

His service forever; O, that I could give myself up to Him, so as never more to attempt to be my own or to have any will or affection improper for those conformed to Him."[3] This declaration reflects the biblical concept of consecration (dedication). It is appropriate to spotlight this word first because unless a person is completely consecrated to God, her service will be insincere or meaningless. Lottie also understood that total consecration required the sacrifice of body and soul.

Biblical Definitions of *Consecration*

Consecration, according to the *Holman Bible Dictionary*, refers to "persons or things being separated to or belonging to God. They are holy or sacred and set apart for the service of God."[4]

In the Old Testament, the Hebrew *kadosh* is translated into several different words—including *holy, consecrate, sanctify*, and *dedicate*—depending on which Bible translation is used. The utensils in the tabernacle were separated or belonged to God and were usually referred to as "consecrated."

God's people were set apart or consecrated unto Him. Exodus 19:6 says, "And you shall be to Me a kingdom of priests and a holy nation." God's people were His and His alone, set apart from the pagan population and worship rituals of the day.

Another Hebrew word, *nazar,* is similar and means "to separate." The Nazarite (a derivative of that word) vow was taken by those who wanted to be a member of a group wholly devoted to God. There were certain practices associated with this vow, such as not cutting one's hair, abstaining from wine, and not physically touching a dead body (see Numbers 6:1-6). Several men in Scripture took such a vow: Samson (see Judges 13:5), Samuel (see 1 Samuel 1), and John the Baptist (see Luke 1:15-17).

In the New Testament, the Greek *hagiazo* is translated into the same various English words: *sanctify, dedicate, set apart. Thayer's Greek-English Lexicon* defines it this way: "[*Hagiazo*] refers to things which on account of some connection with God possess a certain distinction and claim to reverence as places sacred to God which are not be profaned."[5] An example of this usage is found in Acts 7:33 when Stephen described how God told Moses to take off his shoes because he was standing on holy ground. The same idea is found in Acts 13:2 when the Holy Spirit said to the church, "Now separate to Me Barnabas and Saul for the work to which I have called them." Separation from the world for the exclusive use of God's purposes is the essence of consecration.

This idea of total consecration in Scripture is always connected with God's purposes. God has chosen to use people to accomplish His work in this world, and we know that "all have sinned" (Romans 3:23). Therefore, we must each be consecrated or dedicated wholly to Him.

In Moses' sermon to the Israelites in Deuteronomy 4, he continually repeated this truth: God's people should be consecrated to Him. "But from there you will seek the LORD your God, and you will find Him if you seek Him with all your heart and with all your soul" (verse 29). God would accept nothing less, and He punished those who tried to include any type of pagan worship rituals with the worship of the one true God.

Jesus referenced this concept when He gave the first and greatest commandment: "You shall love the LORD your God with all your heart, with all your soul, and with all your mind" (Matthew 22:37). His conversations and sermons consistently dealt with God's desire for His people to love and serve Him with their whole hearts.

However, consecration is not just something dealt with in the spiritual realm. Our bodies, as well as our souls, are eternal. Romans 8:23 tells us that the day will come when God will deliver this earth from its bondage and believers will see "the redemption of our body." Of course, we know at that time our bodies will be transformed, but that does not lessen the call to dedicate our earthly bodies now. Romans 12:1 says to "present your bodies a living sacrifice." Our bodies house our spirits; therefore they must be wholly consecrated to the Lord as well. Paul elaborated on this in 1 Corinthians 6:12-20. He summed up his admonition with this insight: "For you were bought at a price; therefore glorify God in your body and in your spirit, which are God's."

CONSIDER THIS: Notice that Lottie said she consecrated her body as well as her soul. Sometimes we dismiss the notion of a consecrated physical body because of our emphasis on the spiritual. But if we do that, we miss a significant spiritual truth. Take a moment to reflect on the choices you make for your body and soul. Are there some changes you would consider?

Search the Scriptures for "whole heart" or "all your heart." You will be amazed at how often these phrases are repeated. Here are a few instances to get you started: Deuteronomy 4:29; 6:5; Joshua 22:5; Psalm 9:1; 119:10; Mark 12:30; and Acts 8:37. Then read 1 Corinthians 6:12-20. Why is the consecration of our bodies of spiritual importance, and how does it relate to the consecration of our spiritual lives?

DISCUSS: In his classic devotional book *My Utmost for His Highest*, Oswald Chambers said, "I, as a child of God, belong to heaven and to God. It is not a question of giving up sin, but of giving up my right to myself, my natural independence, and my self-will. That is where the battle has to be fought."[6]

A sacrifice is something consecrated on an altar. According to Chambers, what is the first and foremost thing that must be yielded to God? What does this mean practically?

Compassion: The Heart of Jesus

One of Lottie Moon's strengths was her compassion for the lost. In a fashion as bold as a prosecuting attorney, she once wrote to her Baptist sisters,

I wonder how many of us really believe that "it is more blessed to give than to receive"? A woman who accepts that statement of our Lord Jesus Christ as a fact, and not as impractical ideal- ism, will make giving a principle of her life. She will lay aside sacredly not less than one-tenth of her income or her earnings as the Lord's money, which she would no more dare to touch for personal use than she would steal. How many there are among our women, alas! alas! who imagine that because Jesus paid it all, they need pay nothing, forgetting that the prime object of their salvation was that they should follow in the footsteps of Jesus Christ in bringing back a lost world to God. [7]

Lottie's first priority was her consecration to God, but a significant motivation in her service was her compassion for the Chinese people. This compassion fueled her vigorous advocacy for missions funds and for others to answer the call of God to missions. This compassion also led, at her insistence, to the first Christmas Mission Offering, held in 1888. That year $3,315 was raised, which was enough to send three missionaries to China for a year. The offering eventually became the Lottie Moon Christmas Offering, which today raises millions of dollars for international missions.

In 1912, during a time of war and famine, Lottie silently starved, depriving herself of food so that her neighbors could eat and perhaps finally come to Christ. Her last meager meal, given in Jesus' name, was multiplied as the loaves and fishes into a legacy of giving that has (so far) garnered more than $3 billion for missions in her name. Her quiet influence has been pronounced loudly for generations and will continue to be an example of giving of self for missions. This is the legacy of Lottie's compassion.

Biblical Definitions of *Compassion*

When we hear the word *compassion*, we quickly imagine the "bleeding heart" reaction to suffering, which is a surface view of true compassion. The *Holman Bible Dictionary* defines it as "feeling passion with someone, entering into their sorrow and pain sympathetically." There are five Hebrew words and at least eight Greek words for this emotion.

Most versions of the Bible use these words and phrases interchangeably when referring to compassion: pity (see Exodus 2:6; 2 Chronicles 36:15);, grace with compassion (see Job 8:5-6; Zechariah 12:10), empathizing with the intent to help (see Ezekiel 20:17; Jonah 4:11), maternal/paternal love (see Psalm 103:13; Isaiah 49:15), emotion aroused by another's suffering (see Matthew 9:13; 12:7; Mark 5:19), sympathy for those grieving (see 2 Corinthians 1:3-4), and suffering alongside another (see Hebrews 4:15; 1 Peter 3:8).[8]

I suspect the example that women relate to the most is the comparison of God's love and compassion to His people as a nursing mother's love and compassion for her child (see Isaiah 49:15). This is one of the most powerful metaphors in Scripture for God's compassionate nature. The rhetorical question is asked, "Could a mother ever forget her nursing child?" The answer is, "Never!" But even if she did, God would remain faithful and compassionate to His people.

In the Old Testament, Psalm 78 is one of many passages that offers insight into the nature of God's compassion. Read this chapter and notice how the writer does not shy away from the sinfulness of God's people but emphasizes the mercy of God.

The New Testament frequently mentions Jesus' compassion toward those who were physically suffering or spiritually lost. When Jesus healed someone physically, the Scriptures often mention how He felt at that time: "When Jesus went out He saw a great multitude; and He was moved with compassion for them, and healed their sick" (Matthew 14:14).

Not only did Jesus have compassion on those who were hungry, sick, or demon-possessed but He was especially drawn to those with spiritual needs: "And Jesus, when He came out, saw a great multitude and was moved with compassion for them, because they were like sheep not having a shepherd. So He began to teach them many things" (Mark 6:34).

Those who have consecrated their lives to Christ should exemplify

His compassion for mankind in every aspect. They seek to meet not only the spiritual needs of people but also the physical and cultural ones. They are living examples of Christ's compassion for mankind in the context of their daily lives. Lottie, for example, worked diligently to eradicate the painful and disfiguring practice of binding the feet of Chinese women. Her service, as well as the service of countless other missionaries in foreign cultures, showed a holistic approach in bringing the good news of Christ to her people. Spiritual, emotional, and physical needs can be met only by the power of Christ, the Son of God.

Peter listed several characteristics relating to compassion that should be seen in the lives of believers: "Be of one mind, having compassion for one another; love as brothers, be tenderhearted, be courteous; not returning evil for evil or reviling for reviling, but on the contrary blessing, knowing that you were called to this, that you may inherit a blessing" (1 Peter 3:8-9).

All of the above-mentioned instructions relate to compassion on some level. Trying to truly understand another's viewpoint is compassionate; loving someone as your own family member is compassionate; treating someone with respect is compassionate; doing good for someone even when he or she does not deserve it is compassionate; and remembering that God has called us to a life of sacrificial love is compassionate.

Amy Carmichael, a missionary to India, wrote numerous books on the Christian life. She said, "The further we are drawn into the fellowship of Calvary with our dear Lord, the tenderer we are toward others, the closer alongside does our spirit lie with them that are in bonds; as being ourselves also in the body. God never wastes His children's pain."[9] In other words, one of the by-products of our own suffering should be increased compassion toward others.

CONSIDER THIS: Jesus did not just *feel* compassion; He *acted* on it as well. How can we follow His example, as well as the examples of Lottie Moon and Amy Carmichael? What are some tangible ways we can express care and concern outside of our social circles? Who do you know that is going through a difficult time? How can your compassion help you minister to that person? In all honesty, do you have compassion for the lost? If so, is it enough to motivate you to share the gospel?

DISCUSS: We all have a natural compassion for our own children, families, and friends. But what about those people who have made wrong choices and are suffering for those choices? Do we have compassion for them? We may think that their suffering is a result of their own poor choices, lack of spirituality, or selfishness, but does that mean we don't need to express compassion? What are some tangible ways we can express God's love and mercy to others?

Obedience: Following in His Footsteps

Lottie Moon had a clear theological understanding of what it meant to follow Christ in obedience. Our salvation is not an end in itself but rather the beginning of a journey. As we follow Christ in daily obedience, we fulfill God's purposes for our lives. The primary responsibility of the church is to be obedient to the Great Commission and take the gospel to the world.

As a young woman, Lottie was faithful to answer God's call. As her life unfolded and as she faced decisions, she followed God's leading in her life. Who would have imagined that a young girl like Lottie would be the catalyst of a missions emphasis today in the twenty-first century?

The Biblical Definition of *Obedience*

Lottie used a common scriptural phrase in describing obedience, one that quickly brings to mind Jesus calling His disciples. However, before we look closely at what it means to follow Christ in obedience, we need to understand His example. He followed the will of His Father in every moment of His earthly life, "even death on a cross" (Philippians 2:8, NASB).

Jesus' Obedience to the Father

God revealed Himself through His Son. Jesus' obedience to God's will is our example. Throughout Jesus' ministry until His death, resurrection, and ascension, He obeyed the will of His Father. He serves as our example in obedience: "Then Jesus answered and said to them, 'Most assuredly, I say to you, the Son can do nothing of Himself, but what He sees the Father do; for whatever He does, the Son also does in like manner'" (John 5:19).

Hebrews 5:8 shows that He learned through His experience as a human being what it means to be tempted, to suffer, and still to obey God: "Though He was a Son, yet He learned obedience by the things which He suffered." And His life serves as an example for us to follow. "For to this you were called, because Christ also suffered for us, leaving us an example, that you should follow His steps" (1 Peter 2:21).

The Call of Jesus: "Follow Me"

When Jesus called His disciples, He said, "Follow Me" (Matthew 4:19; 9:9; John 1:43). These men left their lives behind and traveled with Jesus for the three years of His earthly ministry. They followed Him literally and figuratively, seeking to understand His mission and His teachings. When He taught on the kingdom of God, He often said, "Follow Me" (Matthew 16:24; Luke 18:22; John 10:27). His original audience would have understood what He meant by *follow*; this word was frequently used in the Law and the Prophets (see Deuteronomy 16:20; Isaiah 51:1). Jesus was speaking of obedience not only to the Law, but more specifically to faith in His redemptive work followed by a life characterized by obedience. Jesus clearly defined what following Him meant: "If anyone desires to come after Me, let him deny himself, and take up his cross, and follow Me. For whoever desires to save his life will lose it, but whoever loses his life for My sake will find it" (Matthew 16:24-25).

John 21 records an incident at the Sea of Galilee with the risen Lord and the disciples. In a conversation after breakfast, Jesus pointedly asked Simon Peter three times, "Do you love me?" Most commentators believe that this was a gracious act of our Lord to enable Peter to redeem himself after his shameful denial before the crucifixion. Jesus then prophesied to Peter what would happen to him in the future: Peter would be forced to go where he did not want to go.

If you read the text carefully, you can almost see the wheels turning in Peter's mind after hearing this statement. He looked around at the other disciples (who had not heard any such prophecy regarding their lives, as far as we know) and gestured toward John, asking, "What about this man?" (verse 21). Jesus responded, "If I will that he remain till I come, what is that to you? You follow Me" (verse 22). It is typical human nature that Jesus' words were instantly repeated, and a rumor started that John would not die. John carefully repeated Jesus' statement to Peter in verse 23, perhaps to ensure that the reader understands exactly what happened.

But the point is this: Jesus leads each one of His followers on a path specifically designed by Him. We are not to look at others and compare their paths or how God is leading them. Our responsibility is to keep our eyes straight ahead on our Master, walking in His footsteps and in His will for each of our lives.

Our obedience to Christ supersedes any earthly obedience. When the disciples were brought before the high priest and the chief priests in Acts 5, they were commanded to stop teaching about Christ. But Peter and the disciples answered with a principle that all followers of Christ must realize at some point: "We ought to obey God rather than men" (verse 29).

Lottie Moon gave us an excellent example of obedience and of following in the footsteps of Jesus. Abandoning her wealthy southern roots—and a marriage proposal—in order to pursue the call of missions, Lottie served thirty-nine years on the mission field. She was fearless, often leaving the safety of the missionary compound to travel through the inland villages to share the gospel. She once planted her four-foot-three-inch frame in the path of an anti-Christian mob and daringly proclaimed, "You will have to kill me first."[10] Lottie also baked cookies to give away and taught children; she was mindful of the daily opportunities to show God's love.[11] Dr. Daniel Akin, president of Southeastern Baptist Theological Seminary, wrote of Lottie, "Here is the power of a consecrated life, a life sold out to the Lordship of Christ, a life our Lord sovereignly chosen to multiply many times over."[12]

How can we strive to be more like Lottie Moon and leave a legacy of quiet influence for those after us?

CONSIDER THIS: Lottie Moon answered the call of God on her life and followed His footsteps to a foreign land, where she poured out her life for others. While most of our testimonies are not so dramatic, can you identify times in your life that you deliberately obeyed Him, perhaps when it wasn't easy to do so?

DISCUSS: At times it is a pleasure to obey God, but at other times it is difficult. When Lottie Moon and other missionaries left for foreign lands, they did not expect to ever see family members again. Oswald Chambers said,

If we obey God, it is going to cost other people more than it costs us, and that is where the pain begins. If we are in love with our Lord, obedience does not cost us anything—it is a delight. But to those who do not love Him, our obedience does cost a great deal. If we obey God, it will mean that other people's plans are upset. They will ridicule us as if to say, "You call this Christianity?" We could prevent the suffering, but not if we are obedient to God. We must let the cost be paid.[13]

He ended that devotional with these words: "If, however, we obey God, He will care for those who have suffered the consequences of our obedience. We must simply obey and leave all the consequences with Him."[14]

Has this occurred in your life? If so, how did you react?

Chapter 6

Shirley Lindsay

Personal Evangelism

by Debbie Brunson

Culture and Background

1931–2008

During Shirley Lindsay's lifetime, the second wave of feminism was birthed in America. Women began to question the value of motherhood and a woman's place in the home. The unfortunate truth is that as women gained more rights, they began to devalue the roles for women that the Bible valued most, such as caring for one's home and family. Abortion was legalized in 1973. Women began to see protections under the law, and legislation was passed to protect the rights of women against domestic abuse, sexual discrimination in the workplace, and discrimination in sports and the academy. The first woman was elected to the Supreme Court, and the first woman was sent into space. Women fought for equal work for equal pay and were given full access to an education.

In the 1930s, there were not many opportunities for a woman to serve in her local church, but churches soon responded to the changes in culture. Women were encouraged to teach other women and exercise their spiritual gifts within biblical parameters, and the creation of women's ministries in local churches has seen explosive growth. Women are authors and Bible teachers, missionaries and artists, children's teachers and administrators. The list is virtually endless of how women serve in the church today.

Personal evangelism defined the life of Shirley Lindsay, a pastor's wife. She created opportunities to share the love of Christ in her life. God gifted her with a unique personality: always kind and gentle, never offensive or argumentative, and one who took a personal interest in people. She shared Christ with everyone, from the homeless to celebrities. If a person walked in off the streets of downtown Jacksonville, Florida, she greeted him or her warmly, inquired about his or her physical needs, and then presented the plan of salvation. Knowing a person's name was important to her, and she made everyone feel valuable to her and to God, calling them "precious" in genuine love. Usually she wrote down the names and addresses of those she met and kept a prayer list. She received many thank-you notes from those she cared for in spirit and body.

Speaking of God's love and salvation was her way of life and her constant conversation. Only eternity will reveal the hundreds and hundreds of lives she touched through her soft voice, sweet smile, and genuine love. Shirley Lindsay personified the quiet influence of the Romans 12:1 woman.

I remember my first encounter with Jesus Christ. I had been in church my entire life and knew all the facts and figures about Jesus. But something miraculous happened in my life when I was sixteen years old. I went to Look Up Lodge youth camp, in Travelers Rest, South Carolina, with a local church. While I was there, someone sat down with me and shared that Jesus died for *me*. He loved *me*. The reality of Christ's love pierced my heart with such joy that I wanted to shout. Suddenly, I couldn't read enough of His Word, and my prayer life exploded with anticipation. I wanted to share this great hope with everyone I met.

What happens to us over the years? How often is the joy of our salvation suffocated in a sea of troubles, sinful worries, and busyness?

Seeking Opportunity to Share the Gospel

Shirley made sharing Christ the priority of her life. She did not want to leave anyone without an opportunity to know His love, and she set about praying for, visiting, and finding those she could tell the gospel. In fact, she once became burdened for an influential businessman and made an appointment to see him with the intention of sharing the plan of salvation with him. She brought along an inscribed Bible to leave behind and courageously and sincerely made her case.

In order to present our bodies as living sacrifices, as we are instructed in Romans 12:1, we must remember how lost we were without a personal, saving faith in Christ and earnestly pray for opportunities to share with a barren, parched world that Jesus loves them. He loves them so much that He refuses to leave them hopeless and without "a spring of water welling up to eternal life" (John 4:14, NIV).

In the case of the Samaritan woman, we know that Jesus created the opportunity to see her: "But He needed to go through Samaria" (John 4:4). Jesus gave us the example of living intentionally, that every choice would bring glory to God and provide an opportunity to share His love with others.

For Shirley Lindsay, she *needed* to park at the back of the grocery store parking lot in order to have time to share the gospel with the bag boy. At area restaurants, she was careful to leave a generous tip, a gospel tract, and a personal word of God's love.

You'll find that God places people in your path in the most unexpected places. It may be in the grocery store, at your church, at day care as you are dropping off your children, or in your neighborhood.

I love to run, and I resolved years ago that I would pray for my neighbors as I ran by their homes every morning. Through the years, I've met many of them and have shared my morning routine with them.

You can imagine their surprise when I ask for specific prayer needs in their families. It's given me a perfect opportunity to share Christ.

CONSIDER THIS: How can you create opportunities to share Christ with others in your personal circle of influence as Shirley did? Think about the people you encounter on a daily basis or the people you already know, such as family, friends, and co-workers.

The Result of Intimate Worship at the Feet of Jesus

As a new pastor's wife at First Baptist Jacksonville, I was blessed to know Shirley Lindsay for two years. When you met Shirley, you knew there was something different about her. She glowed with the love of Jesus and exemplified His character and love. She couldn't help but share her personal joy with everyone she met.

Shirley was known for her commitment to visitation. Many have written of her personal phone calls in illness, visits to their homes during a much-needed time, and her personal, warm way of presenting the gospel to those who had been guests of the church. It wasn't a question of *when* or *should*; her life was abandoned to pouring out the love of Christ to others. As a widow and into her later years, she never gave up on looking for Jesus to work in someone's life. She inspired those who met her to do the same. Janet Hunt, a pastor's wife, said of Shirley, "She has been a great inspiration to me for over twenty-five years since I first met her."

Another example of a woman wholly devoted to God is the widow Anna in Luke 2, who spent eighty-four years at the temple, worshipping, fasting, studying, seeking to serve others, and waiting for the opportunity to tell others of the coming of the Messiah. Anna lived her life in total abandonment to her Lord, even as others proclaimed Him absent and silent.

When Mary and Joseph brought the baby Jesus to the temple to present Him to the Lord, as was the custom of the day, Anna saw the baby and knew immediately that He was the One she had sought for her entire lifetime. The Scriptures say that Anna saw Him and gave thanks and out of the overflow of her joy became one of the first personal evangelists as she "spoke of Him to all those who looked for redemption in Jerusalem" (Luke 2:38). Anna's message of salvation must have been met by both accepters and rejecters. Some surely labeled her as a crazy old woman, yet Anna's name remains in Scripture as an evangelist abandoned to God. Anna's life demonstrates that "the LORD is good to those who wait for Him, to the soul who seeks Him" (Lamentations 3:25).

CONSIDER THIS: In this day of skeptics and "do-it-yourself" Messiahs, how can we stay focused on waiting for Him and encourage others to do the same?

A Personal, Intimate Walk with Christ

We must daily abandon ourselves to meet Him in His Word and communicate with Him in prayer. Our experience with Christ must be fresh and "new every morning" (Lamentations 3:23, NIV). Each morning as we wake up and start a new day, our prayer must be, *Lord, empty me of all that is me and fill me with only You.* Our purpose in life must be to meet Christ every day. We should want to model His eyes of compassion, His hands of mercy, and His heart of inescapable love. It is only by sitting at His feet daily and searching the riches of His great promises in the Word that we can effectively share with those around us.

If you have surrendered your life to Christ and spend time at His feet, He will open doors for you to share His love. If you are faithful to abandon your life to the Lord, He will be faithful to use you to present His love to those who are perishing.

Bill Fay, an evangelist, told the story of being on an airplane in the fall of 2001. As he boarded the plane, he handed a gospel tract to one of the flight attendants. He asked her to read it during takeoff. As soon as the plane got up in the air, the flight attendant came directly to his seat. She asked why he had given her the tract. In fact, she said, "You are the sixth person who has given me something like this in two weeks." She commented that she thought God must want something from her. Bill responded, "He wants your life." When he said that, tears came to her eyes. He asked her to step back to the galley so they could talk, and he shared the love of Christ with her there. She prayed and asked Jesus to come into her life as her personal Lord and Savior. Little did Bill know that very flight attendant who professed Christ would be serving passengers the next day on a flight from Newark to San Francisco. The day was September 11, 2001. The plane went down in a field south of Pittsburgh, and all who were aboard died.[1]

We must walk through life believing that every person in our path has been put there by the Lord; we have an opportunity to minister to or share the love of Christ with each one. Some we will know intimately, while others will be mere acquaintances. The Lord's call on our lives is to share His light with a world that is perishing in darkness. If we have stored God's Word in our hearts and are faithful to the task, God will use us to reach the world, one person at a time.

CONSIDER THIS: Can you think of anyone the Lord has put in your life with whom you can share Christ? Are there people you see as you go through your day from whom you could ask specific prayer requests?

Write their names here: _____

A Testimony of Consistency and Commitment

Shirley Lindsay believed in the tradition of family and the scriptural truth that the husband is the spiritual head of the home. For many, she was an example of a godly, committed wife, mother, grandmother, and pastor's wife. She knew economic hardship at times in her life, and she watched waves of liberalism politically. When the culture changed, she held fast to her beliefs and traditions. Often Christians refuse to take a stand during days of moral and ethical decline, but not Shirley. She stood on the authority of the Word of God in a world of compromise. Her consistency opened doors for her to present the gospel with confidence and a genuine spirit to many people who were unsure of God's love. When Liberace, the famous celebrity musician, came to her city, she waited in line more than two hours to see him personally. She asked for his autograph and then presented him with a Bible from her and Dr. Lindsay.

One woman in Scripture who stood confidently on the Word of God was Huldah. Scripture paints a story of Judah in spiritual darkness. We are told of ruler after ruler who did "evil in the sight of the LORD" (2 Kings 21:16). The nation became so pluralistic that God was forgotten. The Book of the Law was lost, and Judah began worshipping the gods of the nations around her.

A ray of light appeared when Josiah came to the throne. "He did what was right in the sight of the LORD, and walked in all the ways of his father David" (2 Kings 22:2). Idols were torn down, and the temple was repaired. In the midst of the rubble, the Book of the Law was found, and Josiah wanted to understand it fully. He called in his trusted advisers and said, "Go, inquire of the LORD for me, for the people and for all Judah, concerning the words of this book that has been found" (verse 13). They called upon Huldah, a prophetess known for her unwavering commitment to the Law and the one true God, even in a time when others had forgotten Him.

Huldah was not politically correct, nor were her words socially acceptable. She spoke scathing words of judgment on the religious establishment of the day. Though it would have been far easier to tickle the king's ears with a positive pronouncement of God's love, Huldah spoke the truth of God's judgment to Judah as a woman of consistency and commitment to truth (see verses 15-20).

As Christians, we are called to speak with authority as we share our personal testimonies. To say that Jesus is the way, the truth, and the life (see John 14:6) flies in the face of New Age doctrines and accepted beliefs. However, we must refuse to dilute the gospel in order to make it appealing to our culture. Our world is in a state of spiritual crisis, and like Judah during Huldah's day, we are seemingly spiraling downward. We must be Christians who boldly speak a word of truth to an arrogant world that accepts no absolute truths. We must say, with Paul, "I am not ashamed of the gospel of Christ, for it is the power of God to salvation for everyone who believes" (Romans 1:16).

If we are going to effectively impact our culture, we must bravely share the truth that apart from Christ's blood, there is no forgiveness of sins. There is no salvation apart from a relationship with Jesus. We must obediently present ourselves as ambassadors of our heavenly King who stands in loving opposition to today's Christ-less culture.

DISCUSS: Have you ever been tempted to water down the gospel to validate an easy salvation in order not to offend someone? How can you take a stand morally in dark days?

God Uses Our Pain to Enable Us to Minister to Others

The women we have talked about in this chapter endured many trials and difficulties, each in her own generation and culture. We see throughout the Scriptures and throughout history that God uses all situations and circumstances to make us more like Him if only we allow Him to do so. It is vitally important in our Christian walk to present Christ on every pathway. Romans 8:28 tells us, "And we know that all things work together for good to those who love God, to those who are the called according to His purpose."

No matter what you are going through now, no matter what you may face in the future, God promises to work all circumstances together to make us more like Him. Numerous tools are available to help you share Christ with others, but I have found that the most effective tool is sharing what Christ is presently doing and what He has done in the past in my own life. When we relate our stories of God's miraculous provision and tender mercies in our own lives, people listen as we bring glory to our heavenly Father.

We all go through difficult days, and we don't always understand why. There have been times in my own life when I couldn't comprehend why the Lord allowed me to walk the painful path He had chosen for me. In 1988, my mother died after a long, horrible battle with breast cancer. Seven of nine women in the last two generations of my family have died from the disease. The very next year, as a pastor's wife in a growing congregation and mother of three toddlers, I underwent almost twelve hours of surgery for bilateral mastectomies and reconstruction. There were days that I questioned God's path for me, but God always assured me that He was in control, no matter how dark the day or how fearful my thoughts.

In 1996, I went on a missions trip to the Ukraine. We traveled up the Dnieper River and set up medical clinics, provided humanitarian care, and shared Christ with the precious Ukrainian people. On one particular day, we pulled into port, and I was *randomly* (nothing with God is random, is it?) chosen to go to a hospital that was in desperate need of supplies. The hospital administrator divided us into groups and sent us to different wards to share with the patients. Again, I was *randomly* sent with an interpreter to a ward on the second floor of the hospital. As the nurse opened the door, she shared with my interpreter that all the women in this particular ward had recently undergone surgery for breast cancer. I'll never forget the scene I entered that day. The beds in the room were set up in a U-shaped design with about eighteen women in the room. As I watched with horror, a nurse removed an IV bag, supposedly containing chemotherapy, from one woman's arm and then placed it in the arm of the next woman without replacing the needle.

A patient was rolled in from surgery, obviously in considerable pain. The nurse shared that the woman had had the lymph nodes removed from under her arms, and no pain meds were available. Further, the hospital had no sutures, so dirty white linen napkins had been folded and placed under her arms to help control the bleeding. When I stopped at her bed, I explained that I had experienced the same surgery. I showed her the scars under my arms where my nodes had been removed. I told her that I understood the pain she felt and the fear I saw in her eyes. I asked if I could share with her how I made it through the difficult days following my surgery. She pleaded with me to offer her hope. That's exactly what I did. I related to her that Christ had been with me and had given me peace in the midst of my surgery and in the days following the surgery. I shared with her how she could ask Jesus into her life. That day (praise God!) she was gloriously saved.

Bed by bed, I went around the ward telling the women of Jesus' saving grace at the cross. These women wanted to hear from me simply because I had walked where they were walking. As I left the hospital that day, I realized that "all things work together for good." God desires that we use every situation in our lives, even the difficult ones, to share the hope of Christ with a lost world that desperately needs Him.

A watching world must see that Christ makes the difference in our lives in difficult times. In her book titled *Discipline: The Glad Surrender,* Elisabeth Elliot summed up our faithful labor in the dire days, as well as the way the world witnesses our walk: "It is nothing short of a transformed vision of reality that is able to see Christ as more real than the storm, love more real than hatred, meekness more real than pride, long-suffering more real than annoyance, holiness more real than sin."[2] We must reflect Christ in both the good and grievous seasons of our lives.

Are you loving others with a passion for Christ, totally abandoned to God, leading in a time of crisis, and walking wisely in days of difficulty? Let us challenge ourselves to be Romans 12:1 women in every circumstance, interruption, and opportunity as ambassadors of Jesus Christ our Savior and Lord.

Elton Trueblood, a Quaker scholar, said,

Evangelism occurs when people are so enkindled by contact with the central fire of Christ that they, in turn, set others on fire. . . . A person who claims to have a religious experience, yet makes no effort to share or to extend it, has not really entered into Christ's Company at all. In short, an unevangelistic or unmissionary Christianity is a contradiction in terms.[3]

Ask God to use you today to set fires ablaze in everyone around you and rejoice, as Shirley Lindsay did, to see each flame spread like a brush fire to the farthest ends of the earth. "'Go therefore and make disciples of all the nations, baptizing them in the name of the Father and of the Son and of the Holy Spirit, teaching them to observe all things that I have commanded you; and lo, I am with you always, even to the end of the age.' Amen" (Matthew 28:19-20).

CONSIDER THIS: Think about what your life was like before Christ and what it might be like now had He not transformed you through personal salvation. Ask Him to restore the joy of your salvation and to place within your heart a passion that burns for the lost.

Notes

CHAPTER 1: DEBORAH

1. Chad Brand, Charles Draper, and Archie England, eds., "Dowry," *Holman Illustrated Bible Dictionary* (Nashville: Holman Reference, 2003), 441; see also Dorothy Patterson and Rhonda Kelley, eds., "Dowry," *The Woman's Study Bible* (Nashville: Thomas Nelson, 1995), 563.
2. An excellent work on women's rights during the Old Testament is by James Baker, *Women's Rights in Old Testament Times* (Salt Lake City: Signature Books, 1992).
3. Brand, Draper, and England, "Cloth, Clothing," 310–312.
4. This story is © Diane Strack.
5. *The Woman's Study Bible*, 389.
6. Adapted from Jeana Floyd, *An Uninvited Guest* (Green Forest, AR: New Leaf Press, 2007).
7. John MacArthur, ed., *The MacArthur Study Bible* (Nashville: Word, 1997), 341.
8. Bill Bright and Brad Bright, eds., *Discover God Study Bible, New Living Translation* (Carol Stream, IL: Tyndale, 1997), 437.
9. *The Woman's Study Bible*, 390.
10. *Discover God Study Bible*, 437.

CHAPTER 2: MARY, THE MOTHER OF JESUS

1. This is only an estimate.
2. For an excellent overview of the first-century cultural context

of Palestine, see http://www.jesuscentral.com/ji/historical-jesus/
jesus-firstcenturycontext.php.

3. William Barclay, *The Letters to the Philippians, Colossians, and
Thessalonians* (Louisville, KY: Westminster, 1975), 83.

4. Roy Hession, *The Calvary Road* (Fort Washington, PA: CLC
Publications, 1977), 21.

CHAPTER 3: MONICA, THE MOTHER OF SAINT AUGUSTINE

1. There are conflicting accounts of her birth date; we have gone
with AD 333.

2. Peter Brown, *Augustine of Hippo* (Los Angeles: University of
California Press, 1967), 19–34.

3. Mark Galli and Ted Olsen, *131 Christians Everyone Should Know*
(Nashville: Broadman, Holman, 2000), xiv.

4. Elizabeth A. Clark, *Ascetic Piety and Women's Faith: Essays on Late
Ancient Christianity* (Queenstown, ON: The Edwin Mellen Press,
1986), 186–87.

5. Saint Augustine, *Confessions* (Gainesville, FL: Bridge-Logos,
2003), 72. Rewritten and updated by Dr. Tom Gill.

6. Augustine, 69.

7. *The New Schaff-Herzog Encyclopedia of Religious Knowledge*
(Grand Rapids, MI: Baker, 1908), 472.

8. Jennifer Kennedy Dean, *Heart's Cry* (Birmingham, AL: New
Hope, 1992), 10.

9. E. M. Bounds, *The Weapon of Prayer* (New Kensington, PA:
Whitaker House, 1996), 58.

10. See Matthew 11:15; 13:9,43; Mark 4:9; Luke 8:8; 14:35.

11. A. W. Tozer, *The Pursuit of God* (Camp Hill, PA: Christian
Publications, 1993), 34–35.

12. Tozer, 17.

13. Jennifer Kennedy Dean, *Live a Praying Life* (Birmingham, AL:
New Hope, 1993), 29.

14. Bill Gothard, *The Power of Crying Out* (Sisters, OR: Multnomah, 2002), 27–28.

CHAPTER 4: SARAH EDWARDS

1. Leland Ryken, *Worldly Saints: The Puritans as They Really Were* (Grand Rapids, MI: Zondervan), 7–20.
2. Women's Clothing from 1700, http://www.memorialhall.mass .edu/activities/dressup/1700_woman.html.
3. Life in Colonial America, MSN.com, http://encarta.msn.com/ encyclopedia_1741502192/colonial_america.html (accessed August 27, 2008).
4. Jonathan Edwards, *Works of Jonathan Edwards, Volume One*, Chapter VII, http://www.ccel.org/ccel/edwards/works1.i.vii.html (accessed August 27, 2008).
5. Christian Symbols: Fish (Ichthus), cross and crucifix, ReligiousTolerance.org, http://www.religioustolerance.org/chr _symb.htm (accessed September 6, 2008).
6. See Romans 16:16; 1 Corinthians 16:20; 1 Thessalonians 5:26.
7. Hoag Levins, "The Symbolism of the Pineapple," http://www .levins.com/pineapple.html (accessed September 6, 2008).
8. Elisabeth D. Dodds, *Marriage to a Difficult Man* (Laurel, MS: Audubon Press, 2004), 40.
9. Dodds, 60.

CHAPTER 5: LOTTIE MOON

1. "What was life like for women in the 1800s?" http://www.amit .org.il/learning/english/ew/life.htm.
2. John Broadus was an influential nineteenth-century Christian scholar and preacher who was also a founder of Southern Baptist Theological Seminary in Louisville, Kentucky. Read more about him in *Theologians of the Baptist Tradition,* edited by Timothy George and David S. Dockery (Nashville: Broadman, Holman,

2001). Quote found in Catherine B. Allen, *The New Lottie Moon Story* (Nashville: Broadman, 1980), 39.

3. Daniel L. Akin, *Five Who Changed the World* (Wake Forest, NC: Southern Baptist Theological Seminary, 2008), 77.

4. Trent C. Bulter, ed., *Holman Bible Dictionary* (Nashville: Broadman, Holman, 1991), 289.

5. BlueLetterBible.org, "Lexicon results for *hagios* (Strong's G40)," http://cf.blueletterbible.org/lang/lexicon/lexicon .cfm?Strongs=G40&t=kjv, accessed September 9, 2008.

6. Oswald Chambers, *My Utmost for His Highest* (Grand Rapids, MI: Discovery House, 1992), December 9 entry.

7. Letter from Lottie Moon, September 15, 1887, printed in the *Foreign Mission Journal*, December 1887, http://www.imb.org/ main/give/page.asp?StoryID=5596&LanguageID=1709.

8. Butler, 282–283.

9. Michael Bauman and others, eds., "A Cause for Comfort" (Day 19) in *90 Days with the Christian Classics* (Nashville: Broadman, Holman, 1999).

10. Akin, 61.

11. Keith Harper, ed., *Send the Light* (Macon, GA: Mercer, 2002), xii.

12. Akin, 58.

13. Chambers, January 11 entry.

14. Chambers, January 11 entry.

CHAPTER 6: SHIRLEY LINDSAY

1. William Fay, *Share Jesus Without Fear* (Nashville: Broadman, Holman, 2005), 21.

2. Elisabeth Elliot, *Discipline: The Glad Surrender* (Grand Rapids, MI: Revell, 2006), 59.

3. Elton Trueblood, *The Best of Elton Trueblood: An Anthology*, ed. James R. Newby (Nashville: Impact, 1979), 31.

About the Authors

The six authors of this study are unique in their writing styles and life experiences, but they write with a common passion: to present an understanding of the personal, transforming Word of God to every woman. Together they have ministered to untold thousands, yet each of them is best known for her quiet influence in the lives of those she encounters.

Debbie Brunson, who is passionate for missions, serves as an International Mission Board trustee and serves with her husband, Mac, at First Baptist Church of Jacksonville, Florida.

Jeana Floyd is the author of *The Uninvited Guest*. She lives in Springdale, Arkansas, where she and her husband, Ronnie, minister through two vibrant church locations.

Donna Gaines, MEd, has a master's in education and is the author of *There's Gotta Be More* and several women's Bible studies. She and her husband, Steve, minister in Memphis, Tennessee, where he is the pastor of Bellevue Baptist Church.

Susie Hawkins, MTh, lives in Dallas, Texas, with her husband, O. S. She is the author of *From One Ministry Wife to Another: Honest Conversations on Ministry Connections* and has served in women's ministries for more than thirty years.

Diane Strack is the author of *New Start for Single Moms*, the coauthor of *Worship in the Storm*, contributor to *The Impact Bible*, and cofounder of Student Leadership University. She lives in Orlando, Florida, with her husband, Jay.

Lisa Young is a coauthor of *The Creative Marriage*. She hosts Flavour, an event designed to help women realize their true worth. She and her husband, Ed, minister in five diverse locations through the dynamic Fellowship Church.

Candice Finch, a doctoral candidate at Southwestern Seminary, is responsible for the research on culture and customs of the times and is a frequent contributor to women's studies and publications.

Refresh yourself in Christ with these Bible studies for women!

Becoming a Woman of Simplicity
Cynthia Heald
978-1-60006-663-4

This eleven-week study delves into the Scriptures and offers practical, real-life counsel to today's busy women who long to relax, refocus, and reengage life with the quiet confidence God intended. Cynthia Heald will show you that a simpler life is not only possible, it's vital.

Calm My Anxious Heart
Linda Dillow
978-1-60006-141-7

Although many Christian women say they trust God, their lives are filled with worry and anxiety—about their children, their finances, their relationships, their jobs. This book and twelve-week study addresses the barriers to contentment and how to overcome them. A companion journal is also available.

The Eve Factor
Shirley Rose
978-1-57683-818-1

The Eve Factor explores the specific struggles that women encounter in their pursuit of a closer walk with God. With this nine-week study, you will learn to recognize when you are being tempted, identify which temptations you are susceptible to and why, and determine your temperament and how it makes you vulnerable to temptation.

To order copies, call NavPress at 1-800-366-7788 or log on to www.navpress.com.